Unwanted and Not Included

The Saga of Mexican People in the United States

Julián Segura Camacho

Hamilton Books
A member of
The Rowman & Littlefield Publishing Group
Lanham • Boulder • New York • Toronto • Oxford

Copyright © 2006 by
Hamilton Books
4501 Forbes Boulevard
Suite 200
Lanham, Maryland 20706
Hamilton Books Acquisitions Department (301) 459-3366

PO Box 317
Oxford
OX2 9RU, UK

All rights reserved
Printed in the United States of America
British Library Cataloging in Publication Information Available

Library of Congress Control Number: 2006926036
ISBN 13: 978-0-7618-3528-8 (paperback : alk. paper)
ISBN 10: 0-7618-3528-8 (paperback : alk. paper)

∞™ The paper used in this publication meets the minimum
requirements of American National Standard for Information
Sciences—Permanence of Paper for Printed Library Materials,
ANSI Z39.48—1992

En Memoria:

Mi Padre, Abuelo, Nino,

My Mexican Warrior

Mi Purepecha

Gustavo Magaña Pardo

Born: June 16, 1922
Died: December 29, 2005

Nos vemos pronto!

Mexico blamed the ruin of the nineteenth century on the foreigner, and with reason.

—Richard Rodriguez,
Days of Obligation: An Argument with My Mexican Father

The Mexican newcomers had, however, one major advantage over their California-born brethren; whereas they could ultimately evade the gringo enemy by returning home, the Californios, attacked on their own soil, could not.

—Leonard Pitt, *The Decline of Californios*

Mira, el problema de California son los europeos. The problem with California is the Europeans.

—The Matriarchal Wisdom of Monica Segura Camacho

Contents

Acknowledgements	vii
Introduction	ix
A Racial Construct of Mexicans	1
A Land With A Lost Identity	13
Only Whites Can Speak For Us	19
Why Blacks Are Better Off Than Mexicans	27
Asian Progression	37
Mexican Nahuatl Spanish	47
White Feminism	51
$61,000: What Affirmative Action	59
Inferiority Complex	65
Double Standards	73
One Mexican Saint In 483 Years	81
Nosotros Tambien Somos Mexicanos	85
Mexicans Are Not Latinos	91
Unwanted: A Conclusion	99
Bibliography	105

Acknowledgements

This book is dedicated to Lennox, California & Mexicali, Baja California.

This book was written for Matias Segura Venegas y Alberta Torres Guerrero, *Miama y Apa,* Eli, Lupe y Miama Monica. I would also like to acknowledge my father Julian Camacho Padilla (1950–1980) and his mother, my Apache Mayo grandmother, Luz Rodriguez, who has called me "el reportero: todo quiere saber" all my life.

Many thanks to my dogs Simón (the Pekinese), Tixoc, Luna and Xochitl (the Chihuahuas) who sat beside me faithfully and accompanied me through many long hours of writing, revising, and editing.

A Banda Sol de Santa Cruz, thank you for those great tamborazos y sonidos de tuba, clarinetas y trompetas. Your music has inspired me in so many different ways; I continue to marvel in those sounds like an Apachis dream.

To University Press, I am grateful for the publishing of three of my books and for accepting my words as they are.

Needless to say, I would like to express much gratitude to my editor and photographer, Joanne Aartman who worked under pressure and focused my vision like Tonatiuh piercing through the night, resonating in the dawn. A Gervacio Pineda for the editing of "Nosotros Tambien Somos Mexicanos" en español, al hombre que aspiro ser. Thanks to Marcos Ramos, Maricelia Carmona, Reuben Lopez, Ruben Puente and Oscar Barajas for your first reads. To Fred Ramirez, Jose Mungaray, Abel Amaya, Esmeralda Diaz, Amelia Romero and Gilbert Garcia for helping to create the images that go along with the book. A Luis Arroyo, my quiet mentor y Don Memo Esqueda, mi yakiada,

A mi México en ambos lados de la frontera, a culture!

Introducion

In the summer of 2005, the Spanish media in Los Angeles reported that a Black female bus driver for the Metropolitan Transit Authority stopped the bus and ordered all the Mexicans off the bus for speaking Spanish. In Los Angeles, the Mexican capital of the United States, a city founded by Mexicans, Mexicans have been and continue to be subjected to racism, not only from the traditional White suburbanite but now from America's other White people: Blacks. A student of mine confirmed this incident, for as a receptionist for the MTA, she initially handled many of the complaints.

After this incident, the Metropolitan Transit Authority claimed that the Black female was being investigated; the union proclaimed to support her; and of course, the incident was never reported in the English media. Perhaps, for safety reasons too. I suspect this incident was not reported in the English media so as to not inflame more hostility between Mexicans and Blacks.

Also around this time, at the southern border, a militia of White men who professed to "protect the boundaries of the United States" began taking matters into their own hands by patrolling the borders and turning over southern Mexicans crossing to the Border Patrol. Many have supported their actions even though George W. Bush has called them vigilantes.

Irregardless of these people and their actions, our cousins continue to cross the border, and every summer many perish from inhumane racist policies killed by rules in the US (locally in Arizona and California) deserts. Employment opportunities await their arrival. In some cases, employers themselves loan the money for the coyote smugglers to get them across. This loan is then deducted as Mexican nationals work for Americans, often their chosen Whites, Asians at the best hourly rate, which in turn assures high profit margins and goods be available at low costs to the average suburbanite.

Retract to the year 2003, Harvard's Samuel Huntington wrote a book, *Who Are We?*, in which he claims that Mexicans—irregardless of generation or birth—were the single largest threat to White, Anglo-Saxon, Protestant American culture. Mexicans endanger not only Whites but also Blacks because they do not speak their language, English. Huntington also claims that Mexicans rank the lowest in most economic and educational categories not because of a racial caste structure in the US, but because we Mexicans do not assimilate. Furthermore, he asserts that our lack of intermarriage (much like Asians do) is another reason why Mexicans have not progressed in this country. Responses to Huntington's book in the *Foreign Policy Journal* reveal that other immigrants from around the world whether Arabs, Asians or other Whites believe that he was correct.

We Mexicans must respond to Huntington's erroneous conclusions. As a colleague and friend, Jose Mungaray once said, the commentaries on Huntington and Huntington himself lack a thorough analysis with support and a rebuttal. The audacity of Huntington's claims demonstrates the inferior position of Mexicans in American society; Huntington fails to note that Mexicans try to progress. Mainstream institutions, academia like and publishing houses simply ignore us.

We Mexicans are not wanted and have never been included (except for individual successes here and there). It is as if 30 million people of Mexican origin are merely in extinction. I do not know how else to elaborate on such factor. Even in places like Los Angeles where Mexicans have resided for thousands of years, way before Whites and Blacks arrived, Mexicans are ignored. An article written by *The Los Angeles Times* on Inglewood High School's 30th Year High School Reunion examined the integration of students but reduced their examination to Blacks and Whites. In an attempt to rectify the error and gain recognition, I wrote a commentary and chastised them for ignoring the many, Mexicans who like myself lived there and attended and graduated from high school. My comments were published, but the damage was already done. We Mexicans are lifeless in the US. We are dead walking people or invisible live people.

When Bill Cosby made some critiques towards Blacks at a commencement speech on their English, a little over a year ago, Michael Dyson wrote a book in response rebutting and proving Cosby as an ignorant comedian who hides behind his White publicists. That book was published within months. *The Los Angeles Times* even had an extensive article in their magazine.

Yet, we Mexicans have no book to invalidate, ante, and reclaim an American understanding of ourselves and to other Americans. We have no response to Samuel Huntington and others like him.

This book is a start. *Unwanted and Not Included: The Saga of Mexican People in the United States* is a series of argumentative essays on our conditions and situations in this land. In all honesty this book is written with that very intent, for us to—through chingazos—have an intellectual dialog for the betterment of Mexicans and America as a whole. *Unwanted* begins by explaining who we are, but more importantly what makes us different in relation to not only Whites, but Blacks, Asians and other immigrants from Latin America. I am fully aware that we are heterogeneous and motivated by issues such as class, character, ambition, denial yet that does not excuse us for abusing others. One essay written in Spanish addresses those Mexicans south of the border who do not comprehend our social position and the climate for Mexicans in the US. By and large, these essays of philosophical intrigue are also a critique of ourselves and those Mexicans that pretend to defend Mexican issues only to side with Whites at the expense of those of us who have no institutional support.

We Mexicans must create our own thoughts and ideas and not let outsiders brew ignorance and reinforce stereotypes about us. We have major battles to fight, for The Chicano Generation believes they achieved much and truth be told; they failed. Sadly, they merely assimilated; I see my struggles not just against White America but against those older Chicanos who believe themselves to be righteous. Sometimes, we must battle our own, especially as they have entrenched themselves against us, the youth, and our parents—their peers should have benefited from affirmative action but turned out to not be included. My mother is correct to say, "Do not trust no one; there are no friends in this world, only enemies."

"Fred"

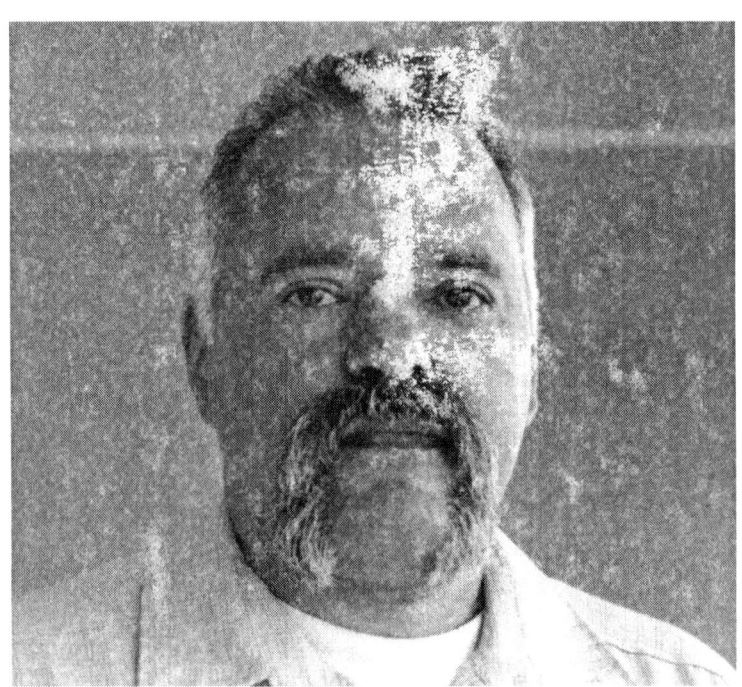

"Gilbert"

A Racial Construct of Mexicans

PART ONE: WHO ARE MEXICANS?

Mexicans in the United States are a question mark because of geography, highlighted by economic exploitation at multiple levels beginning with the border. The categorization of Mexicans by the US Census Bureau is most explicit. Mexicans do not exist. There are White, Black, Asian and Native American categories. My very own birth certificate states that I am "Caucasian," a Caucus Asian who is a Cachanilla Mayo Mexican. I am an Apache from Los Angeles. I do not wear a feather in the back of my head, my face is the feather covered by a nopal, a cactus leaf that informs others of who I am, who we Mexicans collectively are. Thus, the question being posed is simple: who are Mexicans in the US? Are we a mixed people? Are we defined by other characteristics such as religion, language, appearance? Or are we to be defined by media driven labels imposed by Univision, one vision?

Mexicans are the native people of North America, primarily from the vast deserts of the North—California, Sonoran, Nuevo Mexico, Tejas, Coahuila, Nuevo Leon and Tamaulipas grass lands. This includes the highland of centro Mexico and the rainforests of the Mayan realm. We have been in this territory from the moment humans were created by the forces of nature. We are maiz, coyote, lobo, ozo, nopal, frijol, chile, tortillas, chayote, tortuga, venado and delfin.

The Mexican DNA structure cannot be found outside of North America. We are not a mixed population. We are not Spanish, or English, or African, or Asian. The evidence is in our face, our customs, our traditions and in our death.

Many scholars, historians, and the like argue that Spanish colonialism of three hundred years created a racially mixed population called mestizo. I, however, argue that the Spaniards merely invented a mentally mixed and confused population by forcing conversion to Catholicism. Catholicism changed our names, infused Jesus and Maria through Roman traditions, among other violent forces. Many parts of Mexico especially in Sonora, Arizona and California were never truly conquered. The Apaches fought Catholicism throughout the centuries. This is evident in my own blood, my paternal grandmother, Luz spoke Mayo first and later learned Spanish at the age of ten in Huatabampo: Chalea turi cunahuata. My great-grandmother is buried in Navajoa, a Navajo city in southern Sonora. That place still calls me as it once did as I rode through there via bus.

The mestizo is a myth: an apology for being Mexican and a lie based myth. A Mexica is not a mix person. The words Mexican and Mexico are Nahuatl words. The language Nahuatl from the deserts of the north is also spoken in central Mexico: a Hopi and a Mexican who speaks Nahuatl can comprehend each other.

In the Museo de Antropologia in Mexico City, it is explained:

> If we exclude the language, sometimes it is practically impossible to biologically differentiate between the mestizo and the indigenous population. Since they present similar profile characteristics such as height, cranial shape, blood systems and feeding and general lifestyles. This is also expressed in similar cultural behaviors.

Looking carefully at this information, the mestizo refers to a cultural hybrid, a culture defined by Catholicism. The reason the Catholics succeeded was because the sacerdotes beat Roman iconography into the Mexicans at the missions. A Catholic Mexican was rewarded through better treatment and more perks, while the Mexican who remained traditional lived in fear. And at every step that Catholics came across Mexicans, a biblical slave name took hold whether Mexicans liked it or not.

The second European conquest began as Americans "discovered" the West (as if it wasn't already here). In what we Mexicans called El Norte de Mexico, the Mexican North, a much more recent, fierce, and violent beginning. The Americans only wanted the land, and they came relatively close to eliminating via lynching Mexicans whether catolicos or traditionalists. The silence of California is the tunnel of death.

The presence of ancient Mexico is all over its northern child California. I have unexpectedly been called by these animas cemented over unknowingly, weeped internally only to be told later that where I felt such anguish and pain was an ancient Mexican cemetery, a place where not even crosses existed. Another time when I visited this cliff near a suburb community, I was overwhelmed with sadness I could not comprehend. Later, I was told what I saw was once a burial site that could not be developed, for human remains were found. I knew I was taken to such place by an invisible hand to meet the past.

Yes, Mexican history in California is unresolved.

Brutally Mexicans have had to adjust to Americans. Violently and animus. Violence is what keeps California politically American but not culturally. Economically Americans have won this market. Modest gains for individuals, mule labor even for menial employment. Even middle class success is relatively lower middle class. The data is there. Economics is not what I am arguing. The consequence of racial economics on our psychic is what I am worried about. The effects on Brownness (Mexican brown is wide and cultural) are what drives Mexicans to change or alter themselves as a mitigating force to America.

This cultural war is the result of the economic plight of Mexicans on both sides. The war is fought among ourselves along with the dominant institutions. Mexicans working for any police agency do so for first-rate compensation (with low expectations nonetheless). They are merely good soldiers taking orders from the White Man. They have lost their identity, much like the Indian scouts who led US Cavalries against other Indians. Harass Mexicans for "security" is their refuge.

This form of sell out is visible in many ways. One of the most obvious is through reproduction. Assimilated Mexicans who are nonetheless Brown know that they are still viewed as Mexicans. Even though they might have degrees, or a decent income, they are still viewed as recent arrivals (of the lowest common denominator); they recognize that if Whites and Blacks could, they would deport them to southern Mexico. We are the mule labor of the United States and have been ever since the Americans arrived to California and Tejas.

We Mexicans are the perfect racial group. Easily identified, forced to hand over our bodies to anybody seeking profit from our backs, yet the US will effortlessly expel us. Our race determines our class not specifically class only. If class was the answer, then Mexican progress would be beyond many Whites who are recent arrivals themselves to the US. Asians move much faster socially, although not because of their language skills (they are at least up to par with Blacks) but because of their favored status. Affirmative action never included Mexicans. We lived in Inglewood in the 1960s and up to 1998, do you not think Mexicans could have used some assistance to remove them from factory or agricultural field work? We are unwanted and not included, even if we have been in the southwest area before the US crossed the Mississippi River. The US Census data reveals that the average annual income of 30 million Mexicans is $9500 per year. People from El Salvador, Guatemala,

Cuba, India, China and even African immigrants have higher incomes. I am not debating about Mexican nationals who crossed the border yesterday, I am discussing Mexicans from the US, those whom the IRS tabulates data from. Those who have been economically connected to the US via generations of people whom have lived from both sides.

Our racial makeup defines us because historically Mexicans originate from people who have black or brown hair, some straight, crespo but never blond or afroish. Mexicans range in skin tone: some Mexicans have fair skin, some Mexicans have a dark hue, but all are nonetheless Mexicans because of the common culture and the different geographical positions from which many come. Tonatiuh, the sun god, will color you depending on location in Mexico and the southwest, much like the wind currents and rains make deserts and rain forests.

PART TWO: THE TRAGEDY OF INTERMARRIAGE

The tragedy of Americanization on some Mexicans in the US is the desire to marry up or trophy the White culture, even if the person is not culturally American. If he is European who has lived in the US, that will suffice, whiteness is believed to carry superior clout. To be gender fair, I will begin an analysis of intermarriage with men.

The comedian George Lopez says: "Mexican men would never kill a white woman, it is very rare we get one."

According to various sources, intermarriage among all Mexicans is relatively small. In California, according to Mike Davis in *Magical Urbanism*, 86 percent of Mexicans do not intermarry, but the 14 percent that do, which accounts to 150,000 people is still significant enough of a population. Interestingly enough, 13 percent of Mexicans have BA degrees in California which many have cited as a reason for Mexicans to begin to intermarry out. The big question I have is: who are these children of mixed parents? Mexicans and Whites, Asians, Black or Latinos?

Another source—Samuel Huntington who in his infamous critique on the negative impact of Mexicans on the Anglo Saxon World of White and Black people attempts to explain the state of Mexicans in the US—laments the fact that nationally Mexicans intermarry only at 10 percent in comparison to Asians who intermarry at 18 percent. Huntington proclaims that the increased rate of intermarriage equates to increased economic success.

From the male perspective, based on biology (the endless production of sperm), we are not selective about women. As long as they are there, we are equal opportunity providers. We know that women choose us and not us them. It is a numbers scenario. The male seeks, and eventually one female will say yes. Statistics remove the human drama of self-hatred we Mexicans might have.

I have generally experienced that Mexican males marry white women less than Mexican females determined by upward mobility marry white men. As a Mexican male, I subscribe to the George Lopez commentary. White women have generally rejected us Mexican males. I went to a mixed high school of Whites, Blacks, Mexicans and Asians and was raised in the South Bay area of Los Angeles County. Contrary to popular belief, Inglewood and Lennox are part of the South Bay. Whites in Manhattan or Hermosa Beach would like to ignore where their maids or gardeners come from. We lived in Lennox but worked, attended school, sought entertainment, dealt with DMV, the courts, at the mall, the beach and the parks, and ate (even at the better donut shops) to the south or the west of Lennox via Imperial Highway or Hawthorne Blvd. The divide was clear. Mexicanos who loved gavachas were never even considered. Whites would not contemplate dating the sons of their maids.

My childhood friend, Rafael Gradilla, says that the only time you see Mexicans along the boardwalk in Manhattan Beach is in the morning when the nannies are taking a walk or the men are cutting the grass or working at a construction site. Rafael further describes: "Mexicans are the Invisible People." I believe Rafael is a pioneer in this description of Mexicans because he is inventing a new paradigm for Mexicans in the US.

Moreover, according to Sociologist Dex Bryan from California State University, Dominguez Hills, the South Bay is the most hostile region to Mexicans because of the extreme racial economic relationships between very affluent White coastal communities and extremely impoverished Mexican neighborhoods such as Lennox or Wilmington. According to the 2000 US Census, the most racially segregated communities in the entire US are along the coast of California. The South Bay is the epitome of this data. Therefore, no ambience is made for Mexican males to be considered by White women. At times, Mexican women do not consider Mexican men due to their socialization in the schools of California.

The East Side is no different. Since East Los Angeles cradles along suburbs that were once White such as Montebello, Monterey Park, Alhambra, Pasadena, San Marino and the downtown business conglomerates of finance, merchants, government and entertainment, there was exposure and visibility. El Sereno, north East Los Angeles, nestles against South Pasadena along Huntington Drive, a street which is a barrier that makes entrance into the area difficult. If South Pasadena could set up a border, they would. Some El Sereno people such as my mother in law insist that this area is not East Los

Angeles. Solicit San Marino people what they think of El Sereno: the answer is not hard to guess.

In the adjacent county to the south, a place that swears that it is not Los Angeles but could not subsist alone, a similar pattern follows: From Seal Beach south along Highway 1 to San Clemente: Huntington Beach, Newport Beach, Aliso Viejo, and Lagua Niguel view Santa Ana with disdain. Santa Ana is the heart of Orange County culturally; it is the city with highest density rate but also where Spanish is the most spoken language in the county. The 405 Freeway is the social racial divide. Mexicans are racially excluded through economics hence prohibiting their residential entrance into track homes that now average $800,000. Yet when these very same homes cost $70,000 in the mid 1970s, my Mexican father, who labored at a steel foundry in Inglewood called Smooth Holdman, could never have contemplated purchasing such a home at those "affordable" prices.

America hurts.

The endless contradiction in California is the American Dream. The American Dream simply means that a Mexican can be hired at a White person's disposition for minimum wage. Some spaces—even near the beach as is the case in Costa Mesa—exist in between factories so the maids, cooks, busboys and the gardeners can get to Newport Beach or Huntington Beach rapidly. Seventeenth Street and Placencia Avenue which ignorant Whites Spanglishcize by spelling Placentia(the uterus boulevard) are where this secluded barrio with great carnicerias and panaderias abound but so do factories and graffiti. This place is lost, ignored and easily identified by race. Mexicans live there.

I am angry, of course. Hard work amounts to nothing. Mexicans are considered less than, I am not that far behind. Based on this socialization, the psychological forces tear into our identity and survival comes at any cost.

White women ignore us, and now we have to face our own internal revolts.

PART THREE: AMERICANIZATION

Assimilation results from economics but takes hold in multiple forms. Language is a constant struggle. We are accused of not learning English even though many words are identical, yet Asians who speak and write entirely different languages are not stigmatized or looked down on for their at best broken English.

Names follow too, besides language and police. You see endless Mexicans named Jessica, Anthony, Stacy, Leslie, Jonathan, Joshua and Michael, but everybody knows they are still Indios no matter how gringo the name is.

In economic competition, the betrayal is a given. Economically Mexicans compete with other Mexicans for lower paid employment. Survival at the bottom is much more ferocious. Many times we fight for parking spaces in front of our places of residence.

Mexican women having children with Whites, Blacks, Asians and even other Latinos alter Mexican culture both physically and spiritually.

The first reason as explained is the socialization. White men earn more money than Mexican males. George Lopez explains their reason: "Mexican women do not want to rent anymore." Mexican women are no different than men. They want their trophy. They want to be accepted by the White echelons of Americana, and breeding is one way to do so. The guero makes them feel important (he chose her over another White woman), and it demonstrates to other Mexican women that they can succeed.

What I've noticed is that, Americanized Mexican women marry White males. My mother's good friend from the barrio in Inglewood (after her divorce from her first husband) married John Ralston a World War I veteran who inherited a home in Hawthorne. Two of her four daughters married or conceived a child with White men, yet both White men abandoned them. Another daughter from un tio de mi mama married an Asian, my mother-in-law married a Dutch immigrant and so forth.

My childhood friend's stepfather was a White man named Hillman. My mother's cousin Lupe married James Kay. The most visible result was some kind of economic success. After my father died from a heart aneurism in 1980 in Inglewood and the effects of Reaganomics, we descended into extreme poverty in Lennox, while those that married the White males ascended into better neighborhoods: Westchester, Palos Verdes, Huntington Beach and Redondo Beach.

This is not lore. In the book *La Nueva California* by David Hayes Bautista, this theme emerges. Many mothers directly or indirectly have and continue to encourage their daughters to marry out, have white babies, and reject Mexican men. The excuse was the men were too macho. All cultures have macho men, Mexicans are not the exception. One difference is that we Mexicans worship our mothers, thus we are not patriarchal in the American or European sense. Lastly, machismo is positive. We need to be macho for survival skills: for work, for education, for defense and for protection from relationships. My mother has taught me that no one can be trusted, especially other women. If we allow a woman to dominant us, they will do as they please, and more importantly they will not respect us as men, providers, lovers and people. I know this from experience; all humans are territorial, what is best for me. Women are applauded for being strong will, but we Mexican men should somehow eliminate continued existence tactics. Nombre!

With American negativity and survival, many Mexican American mothers have encouraged their daughters outside of Mexican arms. My mother-in-law is a product of this. She personally told me she would never date a Mexican male with no qualms. I stared at myself then glanced at her, and to be honest at that moment, I loathed her. Her cousin did the same; now her two daughters are married to White Jewish guys. The Mexican mothers look like the nannies of their own children, and the effect has been harmful for cultural reasons. I too have other cousins who have married into White families. One of my brothers married into a White "Cherokee" family. White Indians? Free land seemed to be the reason those people enlisted during the Sooner Homestead Acts. I have been to Tahlaquah, Oklahoma. I heard Cherokee women who looked like my mother state: "Hey, people think we are white." They all had Black hair and earth tone skin like me.

PART FOUR: THE EFFECTS

The most immediate effect is that the children many times look White, Black or Asian. All the people I have met who are muddled up do not resemble fellow Mexicans. They do not look Apache anymore. Mexicans have fair skin people too, but they still look Mexican not American.

In essence, in a race based society where an appearance is the sole determining factor of stereotyping, these mothers have at least racially watered down the brown. Reaffirmed by White last names of the European origin of the father and English first names. My mother in law who looks Apache refers to her only son as the gringo Cantinflas. She wants to Anglicize him and even refers to him as a White person. Her neighbor across the street, because she was a Mexican rubia—fair skinned—married a White man and goes by the name Jeanie (I later found out from her husband that her name is Angelita and her father and mother were both from Chihuahua). Their offspring are straight White men based on appearance, name, neighborhood and tragically culture.

My mother-in-law's cousins' offspring do not look Mexican, do not speak Mexican Spanish and have White identities. The same now has begun to develop with my nephews and niece in Oklahoma. Their names are Lewis, Matthew, and Dailee, they are not bilingual. Even my brother states because of location, it is difficult to raise them as Mexicans. The younger one, Matthew, once asked my mother why she did not speak good English in the mind of a four year old. If he only knew his Apache grandfather who was bilingual yet intentionally never spoke English as a way of fighting Americanization. My father must be turning in his grave.

I have other nephews who now live in Maine. They too do not think of themselves as Apache either. This cousin of mine is the eldest daughter of my father's older sister who is mentally handicap and lives in Mexicali, Baja California. Her two sons' names are Butch and Cory Davis. Those are not Mexican names. My cousin feels culturally trapped in Maine. She attempted to return to only find herself in the poorest county in California, the Imperial Valley, unable to find employment even though she is bilingual.

The same occurred with my friend's ex-sister in law. She married a Black man, had five children and none of the children think of themselves as Mexican. Because they all look Black, they see themselves as Black as many Black Puerto Ricans, Cubans or Panamanians do. When they become socialized, as Americans, they construct Blackness as part of their Puerto Ricanness.

The same occurs when Mexicans marry Central Americans or other South Americans. They are not as faithful to being Mexican, because they are culturally divided. Other Latinos also begin to internalize the animosity towards Mexicans and in some cases, they hate their Mexican side especially if the father was Mexican. I see this quite frequently in the classroom. This runs counter to being Mexican, which is of the utmost value we carry. I am who I am because I am Mexicano, there is no substitute.

This misdirection originates in wanting a better economic condition. In marriage, children and eventually suburbia, the end result of mixed Mexicans has been a White identity which from a Mexican perspective is such as embracing our conqueror. Suburbs by definition are White; white culture is then the law of the land which in California means not Mexican. The socialization of the family and the neighborhood is dominated by Gringoness that the palomilla characteristic takes hold culturally. One wants to look like the neighbor and the talk like the neighbor.

Suburbs kill Mexican culture. Maki Kuwano (a doctoral student from Japan) discovered in her research that Chicanos that live in suburbs are the ones who have the least identity in being Mexican. For all the social challenges a barrio faces, one of the positive virtues besides panaderias and great restaurants is that barrios preserve Mexican identity. My best friend Ruben Lopez is a third generation Mexican; his grandmother was born in Los Angeles and his father is Native American. He is proud of having been born and raised on Folsom Street in East Los Angeles. He will not move from there and simultaneously has to persevere from racism and the only opportunity allotted which he calls "Bracero Work." He might be bilingual, have served in the military, be a certified plumber and electrician, have completed 40 college units but he still lives in poverty because of inconsistent employment and internal warring with other Mexicans both in employment site and the family.

Thus, I would argue that because of a different racial father or mother, culture, right of entry, and White socialization that mixed Mexicans are not Mexican. They are what their mother set out to do, not be Mexicans. To be Mexican is racial and cultural, but in the US, cultural maturity has not occurred, and hence we are wedged in the racial paradigm. Mexicans are not people who wear White hats for their White friends and then want to return to being Mexican. We cannot stop being Mexican, there is no such identity as a half Mexican. Those people have become White Americans, and the system knows this.

White institutions exploit this mixing. People in power will hire White persons because they can pretend to be diverse based on the last name even though that person does not look Mexican or speak Mexican Spanish. This is institutional racism.

East Los Angeles College fits this profile. The Los Angeles Community College District will hire Ernest Moreno to be the president at the campus even though he does not speak Spanish, has blue eyes and hates his Mexican side. He fits their profile, yet when he has applied to be the Chancellor, he was chosen over twice. Even he is a White person who can pass for a Mexican.

Not even names can define Mexicans. Spanish names on Mexicans are just that, Spanish. Filipinos and other people have Spanish names. Spanish names do not determine Mexicanness. The name issue occurs in the Chicano Studies department at East Los Angeles College. A White woman named Sybil Venegas who is divisive, cunning, making unsubstantiated sexual harassment accusations claims to be Mexican yet is Greek. Her married name qualifies her? *Chingando* does not qualify you to be Mexican. Her mother is Mexican and father was Greek. Her last name is Coculos. She manifests the anti-Mexican sentiment in making stereotypical comments about Mexican culture. Enough students have made those comments to me that warrant an analysis of why these White people are placed in positions instead of we Mexicans who could have a positive influence over Mexican students. The end result has been catastrophic. Americanization at its best, a form of domination and control.

Furthermore, when I was at Golden West College, I met the president, a Spaniard who somehow claimed affinity to Mexicans because he taught at Lincoln High School in the East Side. He mentioned to me that he hired a person for a management position who was White and was more encouraged when the person told him he was half Latino. Ken Iglesias mentioned excitedly that this person fit a great description. I taught one class, and I was out the door from this campus.

And even Blacks in positions of power exploit this dynamic. At California State University, Dominguez Hills, the former dean Selaisse Williams hired a white woman named Irene Vazquez whose real name is Irene Morris as the chair of the Chicano Studies Department over the more qualified and senior candidate, Antonio Rios Bustamante. Antonio Rios Bustamante is a Chicano Historian with a thirty-year academic and administrative record. Irene Morris did not even apply for the Chair position; she had applied for a position in History and did not even teach Chicano Studies at her previous employment place, East Los Angeles College. The dean wanted to control, and he did so by hiring a White woman.

There is no such notion of a Mexican who is a half person. This is a myth, a fiction; they are what their mothers set out to become, White.

Who we are matters. Racially and culturally. Mexican nationals do not even consider full blooded Mexicans from the US who do not speak Spanish or listen to rancheras, norteñas, banda, rocnespañol or have animosity towards Mexico to be Mexicans. You love having the cactus on that forehead because you know who you are. Unequivocally Mexican!

The spirit matters, but the rest of the United States is not ready for the spirit to flourish. We must fight for survival because we are not wanted, even among our own. The true Mexicans will always be looked over in favor of a White person who might have a similar last name. We are not the same.

Lastly, this does not mean we do all agree. I would argue that Mexicans are heavily character based people, and on personalities, we will differ especially if certain Mexicans want to hide behind institutions for their own aggrandizement.

Futuristically thinking, we Mexicans do not want to end up like Cherokees, White people claiming heritage with tattooed tribal armbands. Blond hair, blue eye Native people are the most evil fiction come true. We were born with brown hue skin and black hair; we must propagate the future with a resemblance of the past.

"Nopales Growing Naturally"

A Land with a Lost Identity

Quite frequently, we hear that California is America, love it or leave it, which in turn affects the Mexican psychic for those of us born and raised here. Mexicans in the US do not want to become Americanized, Mexicans do not want to assimilate, and Mexicans do not want to speak English—the criticism is endless. There are scholars who say that Los Angeles is not Mexico City, it is an Anglo city; however, these scholars fail to archive far enough back, Mexican Los Angeles existed centuries before Whites moved in. Others say that Mexicans are the ambiguous minority.

Recently, the mammoth of foreign policy who had written about Arabs is somehow now expert on Mexicans in the US. In reality, this expert writes in defense of Anglo Saxon values. In his Anglo Saxon values, he includes English speaking Blacks and how they are discriminated for speaking English in their country, but I can never really tell if he is writing about east of the Mississippi or west, because Blacks don't really exist in large enough numbers in the Mexican north.

Does this expert, Samuel Huntington, not know that Cholos utilize their Anglo Saxon writing skills by spraying painting in old English font? It was all over Inglewood and Lennox and most Mexican neighborhoods that I went through as a teenager. There was an Inglewood x 13, Tepa, Culver City 13, Venice 13, and Santa Monica x 13, but there they get too complicated. Mexicans did hold onto their Anglo Saxon writing skills. He must not know how to read in old English font.

The US federal government is partially responsible for this too. I am old enough to have seen how census categories change every decade. George Lopez, the comedian, is right when he explains that in the 1970s, Mexicans were other. Then, the "Hispanic" category somehow appeared on application forms. However, in my household and on the streets, I had heard Mexican through the grandparents, even from the one grandmother who was born in Inglewood in 1915 before Whites moved in. Always Mexicans pero pochos from those born south of the border: we were pochos because we were born in California. Almost Mexicans, not quite, too much gringo in us. Once in a while, the word Chicano came out, but Mexicans still lingered.

Then all of a sudden, the word Latino was added in, and by the early 1990, mass confusion set in. Even other Mexicans, especially educated ones, have fallen prey to the easy categorization of Black and White, by lumping all these different brown people together (some are Black and Spanish-speaking). Though, these very same brown and Spanish-speaking (wordage and accents vary according to origin) people attempt to tell everybody what they are: Puerto Rican, Salvadorian, Guatemalan, and Cuban. Yet, nobody listens.

This confusion is even confounded when one realizes that Mexicans under the flag of "Hispanica" are considered Caucasian. Whatever the fuck that means? My family is not from Asia, or the Caucus region? Where is that place? We are from California. How can Mexicans, Native Americans with biblical slave names, be considered White, Latino or Hispanic? Is their identity based on the previous colonizer? Since when does one continent assume the identity of the colonizer? Are the Indians, South Africans and Irish English because England controlled them for centuries?

The US government does not want to alarm the US citizens from those provincial superstitious paganistic towns that America is partially brown, especially in the Pacific Coast in the and Southwest. Therefore, in order for the US Census Bureau to function as mandated in the constitution, it keeps accounts for Mexicans as White people and not as an additional single category. After all, adding the appropriate category would not be difficult.

As a result, the US Census states that 70 percent of the country is still White. However, it fails to tell us that 30 million of those so called "Whites" are Mexicans. The truth reduces the numbers by 12 percent, which drops the total White population to 58 percent. Another secret of the Bureau is Mexicans for all kinds of reasons also state White on their application forms or other, which would probably drop this number down to maybe 55 percent.

The overall category of "White" is misleading. Like all these so called Whites are one ethnicity. Lumping enemies like Germans and Russians or Italians and British is quite comical and nonsensical. What do the English and Irish have in common? Colonialism? My favorite is that Armenians are considered Whites when they are straight Arabs, some of them Persian or Syrian. Let's be logical.

If the US Census was categorized by regions, then in the Southwest, Mexicans would jump from a total of 12 percent nationwide to 50 percent in California, 40 percent in Texas, 60 percent in Nuevo Mexico, 40 percent in Arizona. Combine those numbers, then all of a sudden Mexicans account for maybe 70 percent of the populous in the Southwest. If combined with the Mexican national north, instantly this number could reach 90 percent. It is all a matter of interpretation and how people interpret data. Daily crossers in Mexicali and Tijuana who work on in Calexico and San Diego must also be counted. Many crossers are US citizens and residents who have no fear of INS harassment because they know their rights, practice such movement in one region daily but are divided by the wall that separates a rich neighborhood from a poor one. A White wall that keeps Brown people out.

The origin of such confusion for Mexicans comes from the moment the USA overran northern Mexico, placed a flag, and called the geography "America." California, Texas, Arizona, Colorado, and Nuevo Mexico are not "America." Natives and ancient maps view America as a continental designation: therefore, "America" includes all of the above listed states and Mexico.

Just because a foreign flag flies over this space does not mean that this is George Washington country.

Geography is the best indicator: California runs north down south and south up north. The winds, the dustiness, the nopales, the cactuses that grow naturally on hillsides, the dry chamizos, the yerba buena that grows naturally where developers have not bulldozed are all indicators that California never stopped being Mexico.

And the desert. Americans from the East Coast never knew the desert until they crossed into Northern Mexico beginning in Tejas up to the Pacific. There are no coyotes or saguaros or rio Colorado in Ohio or Pennsylvania. Are we to believe that George Washington and Thomas Jefferson ate tacos? Furthermore, people misunderstand that Mexico is an artificial construct similar to the US. The country developed like the US but via the Spaniards. What links Mexico are these different geographies and cultures that are all part of the Yuto Aztecan world—a world that existed for millenniums before any Christian Catholic pagan ever stepped on the continent of Mexico.

Many people forget that most Mexicans from California and Nuevo Mexico remained in their pueblos and rancherias. And just because the US flew their flag did not mean that the Mexican in these people was pushed out. How could it? Even if you take away their land, the only way to eliminate their Mexicanness would be to kill them. And while many were killed many, many others survived. I consider Hopi, Yaki, Apache, Navajos, Chumash, and Yumans all Mexicans culturally excluding Catholicism (Catholicism is foreign to Mexicans even if some believe it is cultural). They were all Mexicanos until 1848 politically and culturally. Why would they change? Why should they change? Why would they want to join a group of violent land thieves who destroyed and disrespected their land, who took their children and killed them? Their lack of incorporation could have fooled me.

Even more, when Hopis and Mexicans speak each one in his own tongue, each one is comprehended by the other; the Hopis language is Nahuatl. What more proof do I need? Architectural evidence? I spent my summers of my youth living in an adobe home in the Imperial Valley on the outskirts of Mexicali on the route to San Felipe. The same adobe structures exist in Taos and Acoma. They are identical turquoise colors. Even the way my ama's dirt floors were watered to keep the dust down.

Moreover, Mexico exists in California in other subtle ways. Mexican food, for instance, is the traditional plate of California: burritos, tacos, frijoles, mole, carne asada and menudo. The burrito comes from the large tortilla Mexicans in California and Sonora have made for generations. The burrito is really a large flour taco. Some people look down on the rice and lettuce stuffed (as I do), but the original burrito at least the size of the tortilla is true with carne or frijoles inside. I have traveled through all of Central America, and into the Andes of Bolivia, Peru and Argentina, and no where else do I find burritos or tacos. Only one region, so called two countries, Mexico and the Southwest of the US, has this food. I have been to Oklahoma and Kansas City, and in that part of the US, I did not find a taco. Once in Texas, I could smell the comal. Tacos are as Californian as the coastline. My friend John Caldwell who studied law at the University of Texas mentioned that he was shocked to have met a Black guy from New Jersey who asked him what was a "tall coo." John, a Mexican Black from Los Angeles, was amazed.

Every food group in the Mexican north connects to Mexico culturally. Barbecue sauce, a tomatoe-based sauce or gravy, is simply a kind of mole. Cowboys are white people dressed like Mexican vaqueros. Chiles, add a spicy flavor. Even my brother's mother-in-law from Oklahoma surprised me when I asked her about the food in Canada; she responded by saying, "Their food is bland, it is not spicy like ours" (in her southern twang).

The language I have already mentioned. But half of the "Southwest" vocabulary is Mexican based.

Therefore, to talk about Mexicans in California or Tejas as not assimilating to the culture is rather absurd and comical. How can we change to the culture of the geography if that already is the culture of the geography? Mexicans are already assimilated to California, for they are and were already Californian. In all honesty, outsiders from the American East Coast have never really come to accept that they are in Northern Mexico and have steadfastly refused to acknowledge the Mexican identity of California, unless they want minimum wage labor.

Whites, European immigrants, along with Blacks and some self-denying Mexicans massacre the language. Asians I perceive are probably the most confused. They thought they were coming to America via the airport only to find out they needed to have learned Mexican Spanish much more than English. They needed English if they moved to Boston or Chicago but not in Los Angeles. Even in San Francisco, they need some español at least to not sound idiotic.

But no, Whites in California want to reinvent Midwest America while they continue to use Rancho names. These Ranchos existed prior to 1776. Rancho Santa Fe, Rancho Cucamonga, Rancho Palos Verdes, Rancho Santa Margarita, maybe we should call the state Rancho California. Los Angeles by all accounts is made of many ranchos they call suburbs. They sometimes even try to use the corral as a fence but will not permit chickens as pets. A real rancho has an outhouse, a beehive, un gallinero, some cochis and many chickens. They want part of the identity but not all of it. Life does not function in such way. The body generally needs all organs functioning to not be considered handicap or dead.

California is not some American model of blue eyes with blond hair. It is dark brown with black hair and chocolate skin. The powers that be can build the Disney Music Center, which seems more like a fancy metal scrap yard and a cathedral, which seems more like a fancy adobe. They can house the fanciest Salvation Army swapmeet in reference of their ancestral homeland, and yet the cactus garden seems to be the most impressive aspect of the make believe American Tosh Majal on the hill.

No matter how much California is "de-Mexicanizied," it seems that the identity crisis is really in those Whites and Blacks who believe that somehow, some way America remained east of the Mississippi and left them in Northern Mexico.

For Mexicans with the identity crisis, it is not your fault. All you need to do is feel the sun, and see the dust pass you. View the browning of the chamizos, and keep enjoying the tacos, for that tells you that you live in the Northern Mexican state of California.

"Rows of Published Books"

Only Whites Can Speak For US

As a Mexican from the US, a teacher, an author, and a critic, I have come to notice a suicidal tendency that American society has imposed on Mexicans. One such tendency that I find to be the most insulting is: when outsiders write about Mexicans subjectively. When a White female writes and publishes a Mexican cookbook, where should the oxymoron begin?

Contrary to popular belief and the false perceptions from the English departments, all literature is subjective. Thus in keeping in such tradition, I am stating the point that in the US, only Whites have been granted authorship (both fiction and non-fiction) on Mexicans, many times erroneously. The result remains and has had a lasting effect.

Now do not misunderstand me. I do believe that there are two ways of writing books within the realm of Mexicans. The first way Mexicans in American society are analyzed is through the group of authors that study the Anglo power structure such as Carey McWilliams, Mike Davis, William Deverell and even Neil Foley (His mother is Mexican, but names carry much weight, and in his case, he does not identify himself as Neil Foley Trejo.). These authors have studied and written about the impact White Power has had on Mexicans but through blue eyes. These authors are writing about what Whites across the board have done to advance, progress, manipulate, develop, improve, expand, enlarge, make bigger and as an ultimate means acquire wealth. The fact that Mexicans are the victims of such expansion is more inconsequential with geography determining the emphasis on Mexicans. Thus, Mexicans in these texts are "side-effects" in effect.

If this was Florida or Georgia, the end focus might as well be Seminoles, Blacks or Cherokees. Authors who write about Tejas or California will always have to address the Mexican question simply based on demographics and culture. This is the native culture albeit laced with Spanish Catholicism, but nonetheless Nahuatl based. These authors (and many others) focus on White Power whatever their realm of interest; the focus is not concentrated on Mexican responses to the events or an attempt to fight off the exploitation.

Fair enough, but the second group of authors that drive me suicidal and which I find to be even more insulting are White authors who write about multiple Mexican experiences as if they were insiders.

First and foremost, no matter how many doctoral dissertations a person has, no matter how many endless observations are made of people in their natural settings, no matter how many books a person has read, there is no substitute for birth when writing about a people and their experience. Furthermore beyond birth, all the stages of life—infancy to childhood to adolescence to young adulthood to adulthood and to old age should be counted too. A person or author must come from that cultural home where he has lived the positive to negative, the positive to semi-negative over and over. He must speak the language from infancy, live with the customs and habits, with the discrimination and subjugation, and even have the dark skin with Black hair. Some people would argue that race is not an issue for Mexicans, but I as a dark, Yaki, Apache-looking Mexican tell you it matters, for even among Mexican females looking too Indio might be a turnoff. Plus fair skin Mexicans still live in barrios no matter what color they dye their hair. Even albino Mexicans, who we call gueros are admired more.

In all honesty, I find it insulting that Whites have been given license to write about Mexicans from intimate settings. I have trouble with this value taken and given to them. These authors are outsiders who might be sympathetic yet are able to go home to a suburb where they do not lack the necessities we struggle for daily. These authors are themselves a product of a racial inheritance, which enabled them to attend college in the first place and not have to worry about a job. When Whites write for us, there is a voice missing, the very voice they profess to be writing about.

The best Black literature is not Black literature by White people but rather by Blacks themselves such as Frederick Douglass, WEB DuBois, George Wright, Nora Zeale Hurston, Langston Hughes, James Baldwin, and Toni Morrison. Even rappers, writers in their own voices such as Tupac Shakur and Grand Master Flash, cannot be substituted. As a matter of fact, what the White writers of the past demonstrated when they wrote about Blacks was their very own prejudice of their time.

The same occurs with Mexicans; White writers from the outside write White and obliterate Brown. It is an academic contradiction in the so-called scientific approach of being objective, their subjectivity is their reference point.

How suicidal is this? Today, Mexicans make up 30 million plus, yet very few books on Mexicans by Mexicans get published. Religious Jewish books, followed by Black literature and the recent gay/lesbian White writing has taken hold. The limited books that do get published on Mexicans are by Whites.

A classic example is *The Maya: Life, Myth and Art* by Timothy Laughton. I bought this book at a Barnes and Noble. The information it includes is generic, nothing you cannot learn from the Mexican national tourist guides when you visits the ruins. The best part of the book is without doubt the pictures and great images. As a traveler to the ruins of Chichen Itza, Uxmal, Tulum, Coba, Palenque, Tikal, and Copan, I myself have many of these exceptional images in my photo-album and in frames which I hang up on the wall.

Why am I not given license to write about what I have seen, studied, and come to comprehend? White academic guesses are nonetheless presumptions based on their subjective methods of studying the past whether it is architecture or history. I as a Mexican have more insight from genealogical submissions (also known as oral history) than they do from writing materials that have most likely been misinterpreted or have been given misinformation orally by the locals as a way to protect. My grandmother only told us what she believed was vital, the rest we learned from behavior over a lifetime. Mr. Laughton is an outsider and yet considered a scholar on the Mayans — educational ignorance at its best.

Another example is *Day of the Dead* by Tony Johnston and Jeanette Winter. The first problem is the title: day of the dead does not really translate into *dia de los muertos* from a cultural perspective. Day of the dead sounds more like a Hollywood title to a horror flick. When an author changes the name from one language to another, the meaning and identity is lost. Pronouncing Mexican names and customs in English is in itself a form of cultural annihilation because English is not accepting Mexican culture on its own merits and pronunciations. Names such as John and Juan or José and Joseph sound entirely foreign. And in the US, Mexicans are exceptionally sensitive to the Anglo-ization of any vocabulary or custom in English because the Americans only continue to obliterate many Mexican norms and customs. English imposition is the greatest of all evils. When Mexicans pronounce Mexican terms correctly, Whites look at us strange and tell us we are not speaking properly.

Second, dia de los muertos is not just a one day festivity. It is a two day recognition: day one is November 1st, *dia de los niños* is recognized. This day is in observance for children who have died young, a carry over from the Aztec recognition of children who died at birth or too young. Day Two is November 2nd when everyone else who has passed is remembered. These celebrations are not pagan. Catholic feasts nor do they occur at night. They take place during the day time over tears, cerveza, comida, and the washing of the tombs. Mexicans could write about these celebrations much more in depth and with the spirit of Cuauhtemoc which is much better than some white folks who were in Michoacan taking pictures. Moreover, every region in Mexico and the Mexican north taken by the US celebrates dia de los muertos differently. Thus, no one person can assume the representations are all the same, each is based on its own cultural geography.

There was a book once on an undocumented woman in Los Angeles in story form by some White woman from some press in Maryland. This book was a gag. What would some academician in English know about the undocumented world of Mexicans? Did she interview her maid and then make conclusions because in White literature that seems to be the norm as it is with films such as *Spanglish*. The book *The Tortilla Curtain* fits into this genre. I have glanced at it but refused to read the whole book simply because it is written from a White perspective of privilege and their Mexican maids up in Malibu. How asshole twisting. The ironic part is that all Whites whom I have encountered and have read the book believe it is superb. However, when some of my students read the book concurrently with my course on the Border, they think the book was stereotypical, benign, bigoted, and not of quality; the book mirrors people complaining of a mishap in their superficial, secluded life.

John Steinbeck's supposed classic, *Tortilla Flats,* might have started this genre of ignorant White literature and their Mexican caricatures. The story line of Mexicans being drunk on red wine, preferring to live outside under the trees because they could not handle homeownership is plain stupid. First of all, most Mexicans I know do not drink red wine, it is not in our culture: cerveza Tecate caguama, tequila, brandy *Presidente* are our drinks. We do not even call red wine vino, in Mexican Spanish, vino refers to Brandy. Some Mexican college graduates pretend to drink red wine, but they are trying to fit in. Mexicans do not buy cheap red wine at Trader Joe's; it is old White drunks who buy caseloads and drive away. Another problem with Steinbeck's book is the Catholic focus with San Francisco de Asis; this focus was in fact funny, Mexican men more than their female counterparts are even less religious. Their religion is food, women, honest (the dollar is honest in our eyes) hard work, and occasional gambling no different than anybody else. Even when I showed the film to a class, my students were appalled at the White actors with chocolate makeup to make them seem more Mexican. It was not only Blacks they imitated when they painted their faces. And that was Steinbeck's break through novel? I cannot comprehend that rationality.

Jill McKeever Furst's *The Natural History of the Soul in Ancient Mexico* is to me another one of those suicidal books. If there is one aspect Mexicans know about themselves, it is their soul. My mother, brother, grandparents, and sister accept the fact that our soul is another life of its own. My grandfather quietly admitted that his mother would talk to him, she would reach out for her youngest son. I as a child remember hearing a voice speak to my abuelo because I used to sleep with him in the adobe home under the alamo tree. While I at first tried to fight this side, I have seen my father appear before me on at least three different occasions when I did not even seek him (My father has been dead for 24 years). Everything this woman writes about are experiences I have lived through from my mother and grandparents. I was not even raised Catholic nor any branch of Christianity and have more comprehension of the power of peyote and the cleansing that the spirit requires and thrives for. I have had limpias on three different occasions but only until now have I bothered to write about them, still only to prove a point, not to spread or even pimp my experiences.

I believe these are private ceremonies we must preserve for ourselves. I do not wear a cross on my neck for protection; I wear un ojo de venado, a deer eye for clarity. I am sure a Mexican author would have written from his perspective if there was not so much censorship or White backlash.

Carlos Castañeda's book series on Don Juan and the Yaqui Ways was considered by the anthropology community as worthless. Considering the fact that the origin of anthropology is rooted in English Imperialism, I find their claim to objectivity and educational righteousness as truthful as the myth that Jews are the chosen people. Mythical lies in my opinion.

Can Mexicans not write for themselves? As Juan Gonzales writes in *Harvest of Empire*, Mexicans do not reflect the cultural mirror of America; therefore, why would they be given the access?

The same can be stated about the literature of cholos on the gangs from East Los Angeles by Joan Moore. What would a White woman know about gangs no matter how much access? That is an experience lived and not necessarily by being a cholo but also by living in the neighborhood. Non-cholo Mexicans understand the laws of gangs, the customs, how to avoid others, and who to respect. I grew up in Lennox and lived in the spot where the gang Tepa hung out. They never once threatened me not because they could not, but because I did not belong or associate to them; it was understood that only insiders from other gangs were fair game. In Los Angeles County, most Mexicans could be scholars on Cholos one way or another; I think my mother was the best. She got them to protect her car and herself, respectfully greeting them, encouraging them to attend school, even handing out plastic bags as raincoats when it rained. Tepa responded by offering her pisto.

A true author of gangs in East LA is Luis Rodriguez, author of *Always Running*. In this book, everyone can see his voice and live through his ups and downs. I found James Diego Vigil's *Barrio Gangs* very credible and not necessarily because of his anthropological methodology, but because when he states in his book in the section on cruising, "I enjoyed this part the most, very similar to counting coos." I comprehend that only a veterano, a former cholo, could enjoy carpooling with his lokes on, his compas next to him, and the freedom of the road even if up and down the street.

The tragedy is that there are not enough authors like Luis Rodriguez and James Diego Vigil. Now we have Tom Hayden speaking on the behalf of cholos themselves. The former Anti-Vietnam War activist, former husband of Jane Fonda, former state legislator from Santa Monica whose residents are progressive but only on White issues affecting them. I did not see them fight to preserve the traditional Santa Monica Mexican neighborhoods who have now by all accounts have been obliterated from this city. As Reynaldo Arroyo once said to me, "Nos sacaron de Santa Monica y muchos callimos en Los Angeles, al este de la Robertson o alla por Inglewood y Lennox." In the 2000 US Census, while the rest of Los Angeles County had demographic growth, the city of Santa Monica was one of the few cities that had a population decline of 4 percent. Guess who was forced out? Why does Tom Hayden not write about that catastrophe?

This disparity of Whites speaking for Mexicans is visible in other art forms too. The host of a local rocnespañol television program called *Rocamole* is some Jewish White guy named Josh Kuns who teaches in the English department at UC Riverside. It is hard to believe that the television producers could not fine a Mexican vato from Los Angeles who could spill idiotic phrases about Rock-n-Roll in Spanish. I remember in 1987 the first time I traveled to central Mexico, from Monterrey to Torreon to Guadalajara and back north to Inglewood, I became enamored by the tunes of Mexican rock. I bought some bootlegged tapes and even in 1988, I used to go to la calle Broadway in downtown Los Angeles with my high school buddy Gilberto Corona to a store that housed only Mexican music not found in other stores. I later traveled to Bolivia where I was exposed to South American rock from Argentina, Bolivia, Chile and even Colombia. I knew a little about rocnespañol too from my travels.

Another kind of writer that I find problematic is a white-washed Mexican—one case in point, Ilan Stavans. He writes out of Amherst College and is considered a Mexican specialist because he was born in Mexico. However, he is from an upscale Mexico City neighborhood. He is phenotypically White; he is the product of eastern European Jewish immigrants who relocated to luxury and was able to get a PhD; whereas most Mexicans do not have access to education beyond junior high school. This is the expert on Mexicans in the US? What does he know about being brown in a country that despises those brown people the most, especially in Los Angeles? He has only been in this part of the world for fifty years historically.

Yet, he now has a book published on Spanglish, a comic book on the history of Latinos, and is the editor of *The Uncollected Works of Oscar "Zeta" Acosta*. Why has Stavans been given the key? Is it that the Jewish American media conglomerates can relate to him because he is first and foremost Jewish? Stavans does fit the Mexican racial description. If a person views the book on Spanglish, it is more of a dictionary. But if he really comprehended linguistics, why didn't he write a book on Nahuatl Mexican Spanish since most of the Mexican terms which carry over into English are not Castellan terms, but rather they are Nahuatl words. In addition, Spanglish is not new. Both English and Spanish have a common origin in Latin; therefore, many words are spelled the same and just pronounced a little different.

Stavan's comic book, *Latino USA: A Cartoon History*, written with the cartoonist Lalo Alcaraz is in itself problematic. Latino is not even an identity in the United States. And how he links Puerto Ricans in New York and Mexicans from Texas and west to California is beyond my comprehension, for I have a hard time understanding a Boricua (the native name of the Island of Puerto Rico) unless he goes easy on the R's and L's; they have to translate for us in Los Angeles. There are a significant number of Boricuas out here who have been Mexicanized. When in conversation with them, if I do not comprehend a word, they will translate for me by using Mexican terminology they have learned from living in California.

Besides these differences, where is the country of Latino? People do not exist in a geographical vacuum. Latino is a euphemism to me meaning not "Mexican." In addition, if Cubans and Puerto Ricans do not think of each other as the same, then why should Mexicans view themselves somehow related to peoples who have one part of their ancestry as African and European based? Mexico has less than 2 percent of a Black population, yet they think of themselves as Mexicans either way in southern Guerrero. I have traveled to 28 Mexican states and never once have I seen more than two people together who would be considered Black. In California and in Tejas, Blacks only account for 7 percent and 8 percent of each state's population respectively. There is no connection between Black and Mexicans as there is no connection between Mexicans and Whites, including so called Spaniards from Spain. Mixture was a myth, mixture was in religions and only because the Inquisition existed. And Mr. Stavans is an expert?

The last book to be mentioned of Mr. Stavans' works is his editorship on *The Uncollected Works of Oscar "Zeta" Acosta*—the author of *The Autobiography of the Brown Buffalo* and *The Revolt of the Cockroach People*. Now, Zeta Acosta had many associations with Chicano activists who are now academicians. Why wasn't somebody who had a firsthand account considered to be editor and to write a pinche brief introduction of what life was like with

Zeta Acosta? One person I can think of is the Dean of Financial Aid at East Los Angeles College, Oscar Valeriano who was working on his PhD before having fallout with the director, Jose Limon at the University of Texas, in Austin. Oscar Valeriano always tells me what it was like to be with Acosta. He tells me he was a brave loco who would venture into court with different color shoes and socks to mock the judges. Valeriano did state that Acosta liked his acid, it was the era. Oscar Valeriano could write a chingon account of life with Acosta, but only White guys such as Ilan Stavans and Hunter S. Thompson's *Fear and Loathing in Las Vegas* get their works published. At least Hunter Thompson's works are of literary merit versus a mere introduction as in Stavans' case. Much oral history is lost simply because nobody acknowledges Mexican life in the US

Last and not least is the George Lopez book *Why You Crying?* George Lopez co-wrote the book with Armen Keteyian (an Armenian) and the cultural void showed. Many Mexican phrases were misspelled losing meaning in their very usage. The word *mendigo*, meaning devilish is written *mendijo*, which has no meaning. Huey for buey, which means cow, and the word for pliers *pinzas* is spelled *pincas*, which has no meaning. Had another Mexican co-wrote this book, he would have noticed the inaccuracy and the lost meaning. Yet, when I submit my works for publication, the first comments are always about grammar and words misspelled. However, this rule does not Whites. They can get published, are allowed to show their ignorance, and are not held accountable. The injustice continues and drives this suicidal tendency to flourish.

The anger I vent is about breathing and demanding equity—and most importantly fighting for a voice not to be forgotten in the White-washing of Mexican culture in the United States of America. As life now stands, even a voice we do not have.

Why Blacks Are Better Off Than Mexicans

> Forget Black People ... The real issue in L.A. is Mexicans. When was the last time a Mexican was nominated for anything? When was the last time you saw a Mexican in a film? And in this town, you gotta go out of your way not to hire a Mexican.
>
> —Chris Rock Interview by Mary McNamara,
> *Los Angeles Times Magazine*

> The biggest failure of Tom Bradley was to exclude the Eastside during his twenty years as mayor of Los Angeles.
>
> —Mike Davis, *Lecture at UCLA 1992* and author of
> *Magical Urbanism, Ecology of Fear, and City of Quartz*

From the moment I can remember, I was conditioned to believe that Mexicans were not persecuted people and Blacks were. Early on from my youth in Inglewood, where there existed a significant Black population, I would hear my mother say in Spanish: "Porque los odian tanto." Why were they hated by Whites? In this case, Gringos meant the government manifested by the first White cop near by.

My mother made me conscious of Blacks; she taught me not to fear Blacks too. I did not know what the word "nigger" meant until the age of fourteen. On the other hand, I knew what *wetback* and *mojado* meant in two languages. These terms were meant specifically for Mexicans whether one was undocumented or not. From my youth, I knew that *wetback* meant: a Mexican who crossed over to Calexico without permission. I even saw the word once in a dictionary, *wetback: a Mexican. Mojado* literally means wet in Mexican Spanish, but as all words have multiple meanings, mojado also means an undocumented Mexican en Estados Unidos. Yet, I could never figure out why

"Abel Amaya"

Mexicans would use this term irregardless of papers. I could never comprehend the word *mojado* because from Mexicali in Calexico, there was no place to get wet, other than the sweat from the pinche heat. In Mexicali and in Calexico, everybody was wet from sweat.

I knew at an early age that I did not like those terms. Wetback for Mexicans did not really tell the full story. How about us Mexicans by vision and fate born on the US side, where we wetbacks? According to the Mexicans from Mexico, we were not, but according to everybody else including Pochos, US Brown Gringos, we were.

Therefore, I knew what the negative connotations of those bilingual words were, and I did not like them. Those words meant fear, insult, or insecurity. The migra could contract you, snatch you off the street, break into your house, or simply intimidate you as you crossed back into the US, our supposed home.

At times, I even felt like a wetback because my mother did not have her documentation when I was born though her father had been a cotton picker during World War II in Winterhaven, Arizona, and her maternal grandfather had lived in the Watts area since the late 1920s. Still, my mother was a wetback, according to Whites, irregardless of my mother's birth in the Imperial Valley, still California, just called Baja California and only 90 miles from San Diego or 200 from Los Angeles. My mother was a Californian, yet she was not a person. Thus, from as early as I can remember, I knew that the word wetback was more negative than any other word including nigger.

Nevertheless in California, nigger was often meant for Mexicans too (and may still be). One example was "Nigger Alley" in La Placita Olvera, an area where Mexicans lived. Another example is in Oscar Zeta Acosta's *The Autobiography of The Brown Buffalo* where he describes that in the Central Valley, the Okies used that derogatory term towards Mexicans.

I still cringe at the term wetback or mojado. And although my mother taught me to be conscious about why Blacks were hated, I could not understand why Mexicans never received any sympathy, any historical acknowledgement of derogatory terms too.

During elementary school, I remember seeing documentaries about Martin Luther King Jr., firemen hosing Blacks, massive marches of White and Black people, but never anything on Mexicans. I never saw a documentary on the US stealing California; however, when we went to Mexicali, people would always state, "Cuando los americanos nos robaron las tierras." Oral history was my education. The USA stole our lands. Mexicans could not pass freely from Baja California to Alta California. If we wanted to, we had to ask for permission in the form of "American Citizen" pretending to be happy while murmuring every profanity in English and Spanish to that border agent regardless if they were White or Tejano. I think my mother hated the Tejanos more than anybody. For us, Tejanos are Mexicans from Tejas, not any thing else. In schools, I saw no sympathy or compassion for Mexicans, and no historical information on Mexico, but I saw many videos of Martin Luther King Jr.

Sometimes, I would imagine in order to fill the void, that Martin Luther King Jr. stood up for Mexicans even though I never saw a mere mention of Mexicans in those documentaries presented by my 6th grade teacher. And yet Blacks were sympathized. On television, in the news, in football, in baseball, in acting, in life in general. When I talked to my Black friends, I knew their history, they were all from outside of California, from far away states such as Ohio or Kentucky. However, when I mentioned the history of California, they just looked in amazement at me. When I would tell them that Imperial Valley is in California, they were amazed. And even in high school, Blacks were in better academic courses, in sports, and in the educational material being presented in the classroom. Mexicans were like ghosts, there but not seen. We were treated history-less.

Years later, as an adult, I saw that Blacks were paid more attention to. They were on television continuously, they were in movies, they were in music, and they were given national sympathy. I saw Black doctors, Black teachers, yet most importantly, I did not see Blacks in manual labor, poverty employment. Blacks were the postman and even the mayor of Los Angeles. I lived right next door to Los Angeles, but I still believed Tom Bradley was the man, only to find out later, Lennox, unincorporated county (we belonged to nobody) did not have a mayor. Lennox was a place where I even once heard a Black from Inglewood say laughing: "Oh man, that is little T.J." Yeah, Lennox was one of those ghost places that only got the street cleaned when it rained. Hell, even the Blacks made fun of Lennox.

Most Mexicans were afraid of most Blacks. As was the case when my friend, Scott, visited me in Lennox. He would say, "I'm out of Lennox." Our Mexican neighbors hid when they saw him. My mother always said he was her son too. Hell, I was afraid of Tepa, the Cholos all around me. I would not even talk to them. And still we got no sympathy from the world.

When I worked at "make believe" Black campus, Compton College, I saw Black White people for the first time. The Black President hired me because I was Mexican, and the other Blacks despised me because I was Mexican. The comment from one Dominican guy was my first warning: "Now they are enforcing affirmative action?" Andy was not Black, he was Dominican, but in Los Angeles, he was Mexican because of his Spanish name.

There I learned Black thought was akin to Jewish ethnocentrism. I heard a Black administrator Ron Chapman say, "Those people from Panama, like Santiago, are not Black." And neither was I.

Yet all those Blacks were from Michigan, Oklahoma, Alabama, Mississippi and Arkansas-outsiders to California. My family was three generation Californians; from my father's side, we have always been in Sonora, my grandmother is a Yaki Mexican. Native Americans in Arizona now call themselves Yakis too. I look Sonoran, Yaki, Apache. I look like the land. Sonora by all accounts is eastern California, but most foreigners to California do not know that. Those Blacks were ignorant of this history.

Interestingly, those Blacks were sons of former cotton pickers. My abuelo in the Imperial Valley was a cotton picker too.

Then, I began to realize: Blacks and other Whites from the South or the East did not have a border set up for them. No twenty foot high fence, no questioning of their American citizenship, no white and light green van watching their motion, nobody trekking through canyons or waterless valley deserts. They could move freely. They could come to California and not work in the fields or in the sweatshops sewing by pieces as I helped my mother do in 1981. Blacks did not work in construction as my father had done in 1980. Plus, they could play sports. University professors in labor history would argue that they did manual labor such as janitorial employment in schools and other buildings. I would argue that those were ideal jobs that my mother and other US born Mexicans would aspire to. Those would have been heavenly jobs with good wages and benefits. We were gardeners for them.

My paternal grandfather could remember when Blacks were not visible in Inglewood. Blacks had not been required to hire coyotes to bring them to California. They had free access because they were Black, could speak English, and were seen as Americans. Mexicans—on the other hand—were seen as intruders, foreigners, non-American. Blacks were never illegals or mojados. When farming ceased to exist in the south, Blacks could move to California and have their American Dream. Affirmative Action was made for them, and they—especially my colleagues at Compton College—believed they were entitled too. Affirmative Action meant Black, yet numerically Mexicans were the largest minority in the state. We just happen to be counted as Caucasian to not alarm the White people of California's true population and not anger the Blacks towards Mexicans as if we were going to steal something from them. And yet, my father and mother needed affirmative action. My father was a junior high drop out in the fields of California and would only dream of playing football. He only paid taxes so that others could attend college.

Furthermore, Blacks had sympathy from Whites, even if to quiet them up. Mexicans had arrogance flung at them. We would hear: "You should be happy you're in America." I looked around my one bedroom rented shack for five boys and two adults and thought, "This is America?" Later, I stared at Lennox and hoped for death. Maybe in death, I would find equality because in America, I only found desperation. Even sympathetic Whites had more sympathy for Blacks. If I would argue that Mexicans had worse conditions and were subject to disappearance at the will of an INS agent, Whites would say, "Well because Blacks . . ." And what, Mexicans did not lose their land? Mexicans still cannot make the case for some form of reparation because all the compassion goes to Blacks.

In a 1990, anti-war Iraqi protest at the Federal Building, a Mexican protestor addressed the crowd, asking who picks their lettuce and tomatoes, who has built modern America. And behind me, I heard a white man in his late twenties state, "Because of slavery." Blacks are owed for their afflictions. For Mexicans, it's not the same claim? The fortified American border with its wealth of gold (gold that belonged to Mexico collectively) is the advantage they have over Mexicans. Mexicans are being criminalized for being born here or attempting to come north. It was permissible for Whites and Blacks to be here, but not for Mexicans to exist in California, a state which still carries a Mexican name, and a city, Los Angeles, that has never ceased to be Mexican. Mexicans are just intruders to their homeland.

Notwithstanding, Blacks have sympathies, which are manifested in Black colleges, in Black college funds, even in hiring. Blacks are hired as administrators in community colleges or state universities, as governmental employees. College admissions consider Blacks even though they only account for 7 percent of the state's population. In fact, 20 percent of Blacks have a college degree.

For Mexicans, East Los Angeles College might be as good as it gets. However, East Los Angeles College prefers to hire self-hating half Mexicans (halfbreeds are not Mexicans) who are interested in their personal survival. Outside of that, token Mexicans are as good as it gets, unless it is a barrio college that serves local union needs or an aspiring politician who utilizes fake rhetoric of "Si se puede."

Blacks are immune from the discrimination that Mexicans face. First and foremost, Blacks might be Black and not White, but they are still Americans, though both are foreigners to the Mexican deserts of the North. In 1994, when White animosity reached Third Reich proportions through "democracy" or Pproposition 187 education and services were denied to undocumented humans, which translated means Mexicans (even though half of the White population are European immigrants). Blacks were not affected by such anger; in many cases, they voted for this initiative, but the stigmatization did not linger in them. A Black psychology professor at Cal State Long Beach told me his students were going to vote to send a message: "Those Orange County Whites are upset." He as a Black man did not sense fear. Neither did they at Compton College where they were in charge. Besides, that initiative did not mean

Black or Asian. Now we know there are many Black immigrants from Trinidad & Tobago, Jamaica, Belize, the Bahamas and even English Blacks. This measure was not aimed at them. Not to mention that people often consider those English or Caribbean accents exotic.

Proposition 187 made Mexicans open targets, and this came to fruition during race riots between Mexicans and Blacks. In high schools such as Inglewood, Hawthorne, Leuzinger and even Locke, there were outbursts of violence. At Hawthorne High School, my brother was one reason the fighting carried over onto El Segundo Boulevard. My brother was one not to walk away from a threat, and his reply was a trash can with endless fists being racialized. At Inglewood High School, a Black administration had to cancel Black History month because of the animosity, which surged and left Mexican students excluded.

This is not new. A family friend who graduated from Inglewood High School in 1973 explained that he quit playing football because the Black students were favored over Mexicans regardless of merit. A former student of mine who attended Roosevelt High School in East Los Angeles was shocked when Mexican students from Locke High School in Watts were cheering for them. My friend, Rueben Lopez, explained, "The Mexicans would tell us, fuck up those mayates." To state that there was not bitterness for those Mexicans is to ignore a reality.

Blacks are preferred over Mexicans in this society, making Mexicans vulnerable to racism not only from Whites but from Blacks in power positions.

The California State University, Dominguez Hills (in Carson where the Mexican rancho of Manuel Dominguez once stood and who was one of the original authors of the California American constitution) finds itself in the same predicament. A member of the student council shared with me how the Black Administration, the Black President, the Black Vice President of Student Affairs, and one Black Dean fund Martin Luther King Jr. Day celebrations on and off campus in conjunction with the city of Carson. Yet, for Cesar Chavez Day, no funds are allocated. The sole luncheon that exists is funded by faculty and students paying for their lunch.

Moreover, the Black Dean Selassie Williams (who has since departed to another university) who oversaw Chicano Studies and Black Studies made several decisions to advance Blacks and ignore Mexicans. First, he funded a summer freshmen course for Black Studies only to exclude a course in Chicano Studies department. Second, when he hired a new chair for Chicano Studies, he selected a person for the position who did not even apply and ignored the committee selection (a committee made of faculty, students and community). The better candidate was a man with twenty-five years experience teaching of Mexican History in the US. This dean played his power at the expense of the Mexican Studies program. Had a Mexican done that to Black Studies, the Black Caucus would have been making calls. There is a hypocritical factor in this usurpation of academic power too.

In academic circles, we see that Blacks attempt to dominate the discourse. In introduction to Black Studies, Cultural Nationalism teaches that the Mexican Mother Culture of the Olmecs is African based. Some of their arguments are wind currents, and others are that the stone figures have Black features, "big lips and wide noses." They teach that Veracruz is part African. I have been to Veracruz, the Jarochos are dark because of the angle of the sun and the humidity of the Gulf of Mexico, but those are only the coastal people. Twenty five miles to the west, the Jarochos live in mountains and pine forests.

When I ask the locals I met in Veracruz about any African heritage, they stated, "No, the Mexicans who were crossed with Africans are in the Pacific, from Acapulco south." Thus, the native people are stating something different. Plus, the Olmecs' major sites are in Tabasco and Campeche to the south of Veracruz. In Veracruz, the Totonac, Huaxtec, Nahuatl, and Tajin cultures are found-none of them have any relationship to Africa, unless we count Catholicism.

The same exists for California. Once on a radio program, a Black Historian made the argument that the founders of Los Angeles (Yang-Na, a Nahuatl name) were negros and chinos from Sinaloa. Blacks and Chinese have never been part of the Sinaloa/Sonora makeup. First of all, Mexican Spanish comprehension is vital. Even today, Mexicans assign hue skin apodos nicknames to people. Mexicans always call the darkest family members "negro,"semi dark is "prieto," "gueros" for the lighest. Or we name based on hair: Chino for Mexicans means curly hair. Thus when the friars wrote the racial description of people, they were describing them according to their look much more than their racial type, for they were all Mexicans. I have curly hair, and my mother tells me I have chino hair like my grandmother.

Black and White historians are assigning value in their writings without comprehending culture. Even the Toltecs in the 8th century referred to their leader Ce Acatl Topiltzin-Quetzalcoatl as being fair skin. Moreover, numerically speaking if only 125,000 Spaniards came north during the colonial period, the reality of transporting Black people was illogical when they could round up local people to do slave labor as they did in California. Overall, Black Studies is incorrect to interfere in Mexican Studies. My relatives in Mexicali just 200 miles from Los Angeles don't ever see Blacks or Whites until they come to Los Angeles.

Furthermore, the animosity that Blacks have toward Mexicans is quite visible. In 2003, at Cal State Dominguez Hills, Abel Amaya—a Chicano Studies professor and the former director of El Centro Chicano at the University of Southern California—donated 700 books on Mexican history from both sides of the border. The administration refuses to name the donation in the library The Chicano Center or the Abel Amaya Collection because of perceived racism. The man donates the single largest collection of Chicano Studies books, was himself part of the Chicano Civil Rights movement and a pioneer in his own right for Mexicans, yet his contribution cannot be recognized. Now if Cornel West or Toni Morrison donated books, they would have a center named after them. I see the Rosa Parks Interchange, the Bradley Airport or the Ralph Bunche Hall, even the Do Ahn Chang Interchange, but nowhere do Mexicans feel like they belong.

Whites perceive Blacks as an oppressed people, so they print their words. Authors such as W.E. B. DuBois, Richard Wright, Langston Hughes, James Baldwin, Toni Morrison, and Octavia Butler can be published, but only Chicana Lesbian Mexican father-bashing literature or union based White literature as if Mexicans need labor unions to eat are published for Mexicans. And with anger brewing in people, we continue.

The statistics do not lie. According to *Magical Urbanism* by Mike Davis, the income per person in California reads: Whites—$27,000; Asians—$24,000; Blacks—$23,000; Mexicans—$14,500.

Statistically and numerically, more Mexicans are in jail, and as Samuel Huntington pinpointed, Mexicans are the single largest threat because they do not progress over three generations, do not assimilate, and are punishing Blacks because Blacks speak English but struggle to progress. As if we had a choice in progress. And this is what Harvard University is stating; imagine what others on the street think.

Until this day, there is no such notion of a Mexican College in the United States of America or a human rights movement in California, where Mexicans and Whites march. Blacks leave California because they state that they are no longer the focus. If they could, Whites and Blacks would round up every Mexican and deport us to Mexico, even though at one time this was part of the Republic of Mexico.

At Exposition Park near downtown Los Angeles, there is the California African American Museum. However, in Los Angeles, a city founded by Mexicans, there is no museum on Mexicans.

Fortunately, I still see nopales grow naturally in California.

"Little Saigon Freeway Sign"

Asian Progression

> Unlike other minority groups, such as Asian Indians, Japanese, Chinese, and Cubans who are voluntary immigrants, Mexicans have not fared well in the United States, especially in those original communities.
>
> —Richard Shingles, Aztlán Lost

> America's native minorities that were incorporated by force for the sole purpose of their exploitation—African, Mexican and Indian Americans—are by far the least economically successful. Every generation of immigrants to arrive in the United States has surpassed these permanent minorities.
>
> —Richard Shingles, Aztlán Lost

Asians are the best example that people in one generation may not be accepted but fifty years later are almost considered White people, at least economically and educationally.

When Asians arrived to California, they did so as voluntary immigrants. At that time, California (a part of Northern Mexico) was stolen by the United States. The Chinese came from the west, eastbound to a country that had not opened the door to them entirely. They were allowed to come under certain conditions. The majority of the inhabitants of this territory were Mexicans, be it Catholic or traditional, but still people who defined themselves by their pueblo community. In 1850, there were over 300,000 Mexicans in California. When California became an "American" state, it did so because 80,000 Whites migrated across the Great Plains to the Mexican north into the Sacramento Valley west towards San Francisco. The search for gold was not a free for all, this was wealth associated to Californios and greater Mexico as it attempted to settle itself over political instability.

Californios (all Mexicans who were from this land) had to fend for themselves because they were suddenly at the mercy of the US; indeed, the US really wanted nothing to do with indigenous people even if they were Catholics. It was race over religious similarities, whites versus Mexicans.

The battle over California began as a violent genocide toward all Mexican landowners whether Ranchos or Pueblos; from 1850–1870, Mexicans were eliminated or driven to poverty. The first laws that Americans wrote limited access Mexicans had to gold by imposing a tax on Mexicans who had been living there for centuries. Next were the land acts that permitted expropriations and squatter settlement. Mexicans—like Joaquin Murrietta, Juan Flores, and Tiburcio Vasquez—fought back, but White posies hunted them down and executed them. Then, the White ruling class legalized the lynching of other Mexicans who called themselves Coloma, Chumash, Ohlone, Pomo, Chochone, Cucapah, Yumans, or Mohave. In fact, ten dollars per a scalp of man and five dollars per scalp of a woman or child was paid. Having Black hair was sufficient to have been hunted down and killed like prey. Within ten years, 150,000 Mexicans were murdered. The genocide of California is still considered the single largest slaughter of Native people or the largest slaughter of native Mexicans.

The elimination of the people in California was done so as a way of cleansing the largest threat, socially and geographically. Asians were not immune and were subjected to violence, but the Americans were eradicating thousands of people who controlled the land they wanted. Mexicans were the biggest threat because they had water and fertile fields that they used for farming and cattle grazing, primarily for subsistence. Native American Mexicans had been rancho people who farmed, fished if along the coast, tended to chickens, cochis or pigs, and cattle for thousands of years. This was all labor intensive and much of the American wealth was to be sought in California.

The Mexicans were in the way of "The American Dream."

When the gold rush diminished, the Chinese turned to San Francisco or to working on the railroads as did thousands of Mexicans; both were utilized as neo-slave workers under the disguise of minimum wage. White Americans would not have to house, clothe, or feed these people. Let them pay their own way. And the Mexican begins the process of life under White American rule as laboring for Whites at the convenience of Whites and their terms. Within thirty years, Mexicans were reduced to renters in their own land.

Soon, the Chinese became the next threat to the newly established White rule. Chinese filled vacuums of economic circles where Whites did not. The laundry facilities in San Francisco met a need for White Americans, but when capital was being accumulated too rapidly, Whites began to implement laws that curtailed the Chinese accumulation of wealth. The laws were absurd. For example, some Chinese laundresses rented out a brick building for a laundry facility and the new law stipulated that laundry services may not be conducted in a brick building. The Chinese also become farmers and fishermen, practices Mexicans had been doing prior to the squatters seizing control. The ultimate removal of Chinese through the Exclusion Act was enacted as a way to remove Chinese competition from Americans. The Mexicans had already been reduced to an inferior subservient position by 1882 and had lost most of their lands. Mexicans were the majority workforce and Mexican Spanish was the lingua franca in Southern California.

When the Chinese are expelled from the US, Mexicans in California were not considered native anymore, for Whites stole that identity too. As American investors moved in after 1890 and took over their orchards or wineries, they had to have access to a "subhuman" labor force. Mexicans filled this gap as had been the case from as early as 1860. Americans realized they could use the population they were killing off as their two legged mules. By the turn of the century, Mexicans were firmly controlled by Americans economically, and Whites had no competition from Asians who had further been kept out by the Gentlemen's Agreement.

Eventually, Asians began to fight back. In the early 1920s, when a Japanese and a Hindu Indian sought Whiteness through the courts and were denied, they did so because they had some capital to back them up. The Japanese petitioner had attended the University of California, Berkeley. In all my years, I have never met a Mexican who had attended college in the 1930s much less the 1920s or even heard of somebody who had from my grandparents. The University for a Mexican in California was as foreign as Mars. To further state this point, during a speech given by Rose Portillo, the actress from the movie and play *Zoot Suit*, she stated that her father had been one of the first Mexicans to attend medical school at the University of Southern California in the 1930s. She also mentioned that many people thought that her father might have been Italian. Thus, Asians were able to battle the system more efficiently because they had more capital and letters behind their names. Asians might have been expelled, but Mexicans were used as disposable pickers, terminated, and deported at the orders of somebody, anybody White.

Mexicans have always been the largest minority in California because they were here prior to the construct of the US; furthermore, they have had major population shifts when the US has recruited them and shipped them north. During a government program called Repatriation in the 1930s, Mexicans were randomly arrested, placed on trains, and sent south. Americans were placing Mexicans in boxcars before the Nazis did so in Germany. Over one and a half million were sent south, 60 percent were US citizens. This I have seen first hand, because my mother had two older cousins whose families were expelled and so frightened of Mexico that as adults in the 1950s, they returned by paying a coyote to smuggle them in. They could not get their birth certificates from the southern side. American citizens paid to be smuggled into the land they were born in, how suicidal is that? My tio Jesus was born in City Terrace in 1932, and my tio Tacho was born in Pueblo, Colorado as he told me his story of expulsion. It is hard to believe somebody born in Colorado, spoke no English, but lived in Mexicali all his life afterward. He lived as a farm worker and so have his children now, and none of them have attended college.

The internment of Japanese was a tragedy but was no more tragic than those Mexicans expelled two years earlier. Some families were permanently separated as was the case of writer Graciela Limón, author of *In Search of Bernabe and Song of the Hummingbird*. She once told me: "Those family members who were deported never returned north from Guadalajara y ya no se vieron."

And the truth of the matter, Whites were given land in California that Japanese leased, and then the Japanese exploited Mexican farmworkers. Major strikes in the El Monte area in Los Angeles County were against Japanese farmers who did not want to pay fair wages to Mexicans. A few years later, the US government legalized exploitation and became the single largest coyote/smuggler from 1942–1964 as farming expanded due to water reclamation projects, dam projects, and output expansion. World War II initiated this farming explosion that even today generates $19 billion dollars in profit and employs close to one million Mexican farmworkers either US citizen, resident, or undocumented. They do not care.

In the years following World War II, things changed for Asians in the US. After the US dominated Japan, then entered Korea and remained, they changed their immigration policy towards Asians. In part, this change occurred for PR reasons: How could the US not legalize the movement of Asians if they professed freedom and wanted to show a positive alternative to the Communist Revolution in China? The 1952 Naturalization Laws permitted Asians to apply for visas, move to the US, become a resident, and eventually a citizen. Continued American involvement in Asian extended this policy: Filipinos, Koreans, Japanese, Taiwanese, and Chinese from Hong Kong were allowed in based on US need.

Even though a child in the 1970s, the changes were taking place and affecting me and those around me. Whole communities of different Asian groups were not really visible outside of Chinatown and Gardena where many Japanese Americans lived. Then suddenly, a Koreatown sprung up. Then, the population of Filipinos grew; they were present in places I did not expect and had Spanish names. Filipinos often believe they are mestizos because they have Spanish names but cannot accept the fact that those biblical names are really slave names under the disguise of Catholic conversion.

Toward the mid-1970s, the Vietnamese became the new face of Asians along with Indians and Pakistanis. Soon, I noticed that these people did not live in the areas I lived in nor in vertical ghettos. I witnessed that they were merchants; they owned dry cleaners, small markets, liquor stores, small mechanic shops. Plus, I saw that they did not work as low wage laborers. They primarily hired Mexicans, including my mother (who worked for a Korean-owned airline food preparation company).

When I started high school at Hawthorne High School, I started to meet Asians from Hawthorne. There was not many of them, but they were recognizable. I did watch how the teachers thought of them highly. The Korean, Filipino, Palestinian, Indian and Pakistani students were highly regarded in the math and science classrooms. They were simply considered bright, smarter than any Mexican. However, I noticed that in social science class, the Asians struggled. A few of them would cheat off of me on a regular basis. Once I saw this happen, I realized that the teachers were giving many Asians too much credit.

A real eye opener for me occurred when I competed in some wrestling tournaments at Torrance High, West High, Redondo Union High, South Torrance High, Artesia High, and Rowland High. At these various tournaments, I saw that the Asian students did not come from traditional ghetto schools. Hawthorne High was not considered ghetto, but in comparison to any Torrance or coastal school, we were because we had a high number of Mexicans—35 percent from Lennox and enough Blacks—12 percent of the school's population to be considered "ghetto." The Asian students were good athletes who lived in solid middle to upper middle class neighborhoods. These Asians—many recent immigrants—were better off than the Mexicans that I knew. What was even harder to believe was that they were not stigmatized for speaking in Korean or Chinese. I can clearly remember students from West High cheering for one of their fellow wrestler in Korean and not being ashamed.

On the other hand, at Hawthorne High School, our Spanish-speaking was usually stigmatized because we did not use it as confidently; nonetheless, when we did, we felt tightness in the air. And, our names were always mispronounced in English.

In addition, our valedictorian was an Asian, Hojin Kim. The guy who scored the highest on the pre-SAT was a Palestinian who by my account are Asians from the African continent, plus Muslims also include Asia so close enough. Within months of arrival, it seemed Asians progressed to the middle class.

Once they settled in, the name changes came. In the summer of my junior to senior year, my high school friend went from Chang Park to Kevin Park. I respected his name change, but something was lost; he now seemed Black to me. Another guy, a Vietnamese, left our sophomore year as Jesse Tranh and returned our junior year as Jesse Andes, I could not figure that name change out. I remember when the Vietnamese were not part of the landscape in California, and they were an obscure two-minute news segment of refugees who were going out to sea much like some of the Cubans. Next thing I know, they moved into parts of Lawndale and Westminster, instantly living in a better house than my family did with a two car garage, three bedrooms and a backyard.

What had they done, was the endless question in my mind? When they moved into Westminster, the city's identity changed to Little Saigon. Even though, Westminster had been a city of historical significance to Mexicans. In 1946, a Mexican family filed a lawsuit against the school district—a case known as Mendez vs. Westminster Unified School District. This case set the basis for the historic landmark desegregation case of Brown vs. Topeka Board of Education. Mexicans had fought to open this place up for themselves yet found themselves forgotten in that important site where Vietnamese were considered now part of the model minority. I remember a time when the Vietnamese had not arrived to Orange County much less California, much less the United States.

During college, I noticed many Asians, even those who served as tutors had much difficulty in English verbally, and yet they seemed to progress. At UCLA, a Swedish visiting professor came to Los Angeles to study the major money men (mainly Japanese investors). In my Urban Planning courses, we studied the NICs (Newly Industrialized Countries) like Singapore, South Korea, Malaysia and China. The professors salivated over their Asian emphasis, but I was interested in Mexico, which received little attention except for the one Mexican *enano* con artist professor. The formaldehyde reeked; the worldliness of my education did very little in my comprehension of Mexicans in the US except to be viewed as immigrants.

Mexicans were thought of as new immigrants, the undocumented. However, many Asians had entered the US on tourist visas and overstayed their visits (a practice that still goes on today). The migra do not persecute them though. I have never heard of any Asian being harassed by the INS or any local police once on US soil. They are free to walk around and do not fear being deported, or having their homes raided. I suppose living in White neighborhoods shields them as happens to be the case of many European immigrants who also overstay their visas (and this would include Arabs). Considering that Saudis in the US could possibly be linked to suspicious behavior along with White vigilante groups, they roam without the threat of the INS stopping them randomly or in their Irvine neighborhoods. They have been treated quite fairly overall.

Whereas in the summer of 2004, there was a front page picture of Mexicans walking up to an airplane that was part of a new deportation program that would relocate them to their home states in Central Mexico even though we know the US government is the single largest coyote of Mexican nationals moving north. The image was disturbing because I saw a double standard. We know Mexico is the 51st state in the USA, why act as if it does not exist. The US will deport Mexicans without visas, but it will not deport Asians or Arabs or Whites with expired visas, it will not send them to their homeland.

Asians have progressed far. Asians have done what Blacks or Mexicans have not been able to do: Reparations. In the early 1980s, Congress apologized to and compensated the Japanese survivors of the Interment Camps. However, as of today, none of my relatives has been compensated for the loss of Mexico, the loss from the 1930s Repatriation or the inhumane working conditions in the US. I heard a Japanese American guest speaker who was also an architect instructor at East Los Angeles College state that he accepted the $20,000 not because he needed the money but to prove a point. That point is a luxury to me. I could use that modest compensation to pay off part of my school loans, which have doubled from $36,000 to $61,000. To be able to get Congress to agree on legislation that compensated a group of people done wrong is incredible. When this happened in 1982, the Asian Tiger from Japan was becoming a major financial player in vehicles and real estate. Without doubt, this made the US decision much easier. It is all about American foreign interest, a *show* of good faith. What leverage do Mexicans have on Congress? Zero. In fact, we receive a veto from the current Austrian nigger governor of California on a bill that would have provided compensation for Mexicans being expelled in the 1930s. Mexicans in the United States have limited collective power, have almost no political power, and are the most impoverished.

The inequity is everywhere. Many of the doctors I see have either English, Chinese or Arab names. The best example was when my sister had to have surgery and was attended to at UCLA Harbor Medical Center in Torrance. Most of the doctors were Asians along with Whites; the nurses were Filipinas, Whites or some Blacks; and the janitors were primarily Mexicans. The one doctor who attended my sister was a Chinese woman in her thirties, her English was quite incomprehensible. I struggled to understand and translate for my sister. And to only see Mexicans as janitors is quite disturbing because I know many Mexicans who would like to attend medical school, but they are not given the opportunity.

The same can be said for my dentist, somebody from Taiwan who had attended dental school at UCLA. In the University of California system, the student population consists of Whites and Asians. Both groups easily make up 80–85 percent of the students in the UC system, which is tax payer funded. UC Berkeley and UC Irvine have an over population of Asian and White students while the numbers of Mexicans have declined by three hundred students in the incoming freshmen 2004 cohort.

To better comprehend this inequity, Asians combined only account for 11 percent of California's total population (Chinese being the largest of them all). Whites make up 35 percent while Mexicans make up 45 percent or 15 million residents. Yet as previously mentioned, Asians and Whites account for 80percent of the student body in the UC system, which relies on states taxes to be funded. If Mexicans are the majority in the state of California and are less than 15 percent of the UC graduates but are contributing 45 percent as taxpayers, then they are in essence subsidizing the educational advancement of not only Asians but Whites too. Sure, Asians and Whites pay their taxes, but alone they could not fully fund the UC and Cal States without the 45 percent of the population—almost half of the contributors to the state's coiffures come from Mexicans.

While many Asian students pay out of state tuition which is twice as much as a regular student, those fees could still not fund the actual cost of any UC. As a result, they, foreigners, are further benefiting from this social structure built off the mule backs of Mexicans. Others might argue that the local high schools are not preparing Mexican students to attend a UC, but I would argue that is where the inequity originates because the funding of public schools is based on the property values of the neighborhoods which are based on race of the community. Plus, race determines how income is allocated based on employment.

Mexican neighborhoods have the lowest property values of any communities. This determines why Mexicans lack appropriate funding in their school environments. When Mexican students do attend schools with a large Asian population, they are ignored and not valued educationally. If we note where many Asians live, outside of Chinatown, they do not account for more than 15 percent of the population in any city. Asians live in White upper middle class neighborhoods such as San Marino, Arcadia, Torrance, Huntington Beach and even Glendale. By all accounts, Asians are functioning as White people, not as an inferior minority. In addition, they are voluntary immigrants, they were not forcefully brought to California or any other part of the United States, and they have no historical connection to this land.

Regarding employment, Asians occupy many professional positions: doctors, lawyers, positions in higher education. The former president at UC

Berkeley was a Chinese man and so is the current Chancellor at UC Santa Barbara. Their limited English accent does not hold them back, yet my English proficiency does not advance me—thus fluency in English is not a formula for success. Asians, including Indians, are a solid business class in Los Angeles. Asians own the Compton Swapmeet and many of the businesses even in East Los Angeles. My brother delivers Pepsi to many of these local stores, and he informs me that Asians and Arabs own the East Side, not Mexicans. Some might argue that those are dangerous places, but according to OSHA (Occupational and Safety Health Administration) reports, the group that suffers the highest death rates in their places of employment is not Asians but is Mexicans, state, and nationwide.

The danger I observe is not only the double standards granted to Asians, but the fact that Asians also buy into the negative connotations of Mexicans. Prior to the Los Angeles Riots of 1992, Korean shop owner exploitation and arrogance led to them being singled out by both Mexicans and Blacks violently. Even my mother stated, "The Coreanos deserved what they got because they were abusive and disrespectful to us." She is not alone in this point of view.

I have further observed from other Mexican colleagues that Asian math professors are acting with bigotry towards Mexicans and are allowed to discriminate under the curtain of academic standards. High failure rates are not just based on Mexican students not being able to succeed but on the double standards employed by these new White people with Asian features. Something similar has occurred at East Los Angeles College, but on the reverse: one White English professor regularly passes Asian students easily but fails the Mexicans. How perverted is that?

And as an instructor myself, I see that Asian students fare no different than other Mexican students provided with the same fairness. Some get Cs, others get Bs, and a few get As quite similar to Mexican students. When society positively praises one group and not another, success will be based on those expectations.

A few weeks after the elimination of affirmative action, a few Asian commentators to the *Los Angeles Times* from Irvine wrote that Mexican and Black students should not get admitted to any UC based on quotas. Quotas should not hinder the progress of Whites and Asians because they were smarter.

A little over a hundred years ago, Asians were considered inferior people; now they behave as Whites even though many cannot speak English fluently.

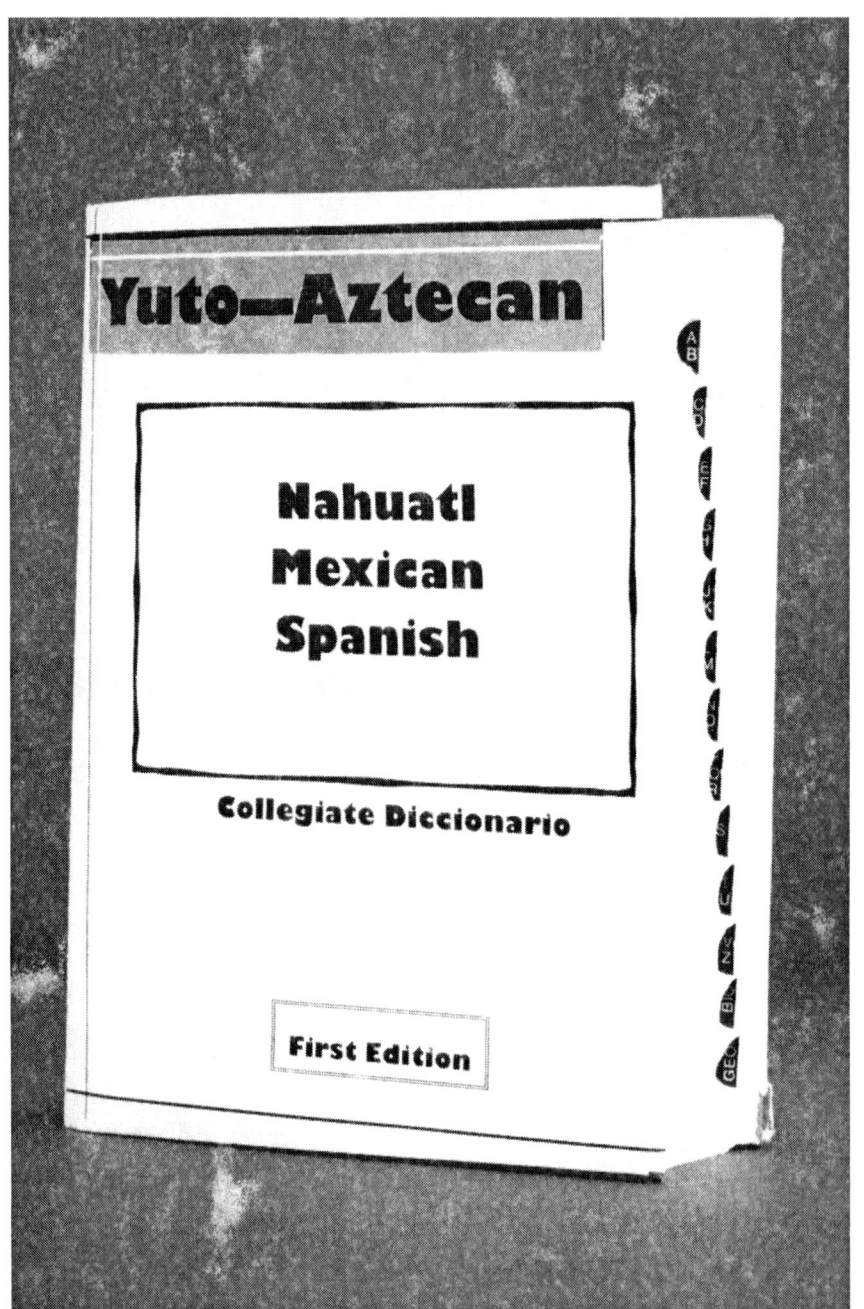

"The Dictionary of Mexican Nahuatl Spanish"

Mexican Nahuatl Spanish

As the British landed along the East Coast and later as the Americans forced themselves into Tejas, they were exposed to a new language for the simple reason they were in a new geography. The novelty of unknown land, plants, animals, and humans on a different continent required the invaders to adopt parts of the indigenous people's language. The new language explained the geography and taught them how to survive. Nonetheless, the British and subsequent American racial arrogance created a feeling of superiority even if only to admit that they were not pendejos. But, pendejos they were.

When the landlords of the East Coast sent Americans due west into the Mexican north, the same rules applied. *Occupied* land already named and established had existed for thousands of years. Within a fraction of that time, Americans moved into the Mexican northeast state of Tejas.

After three centuries of Spanish colonialism, Mexicans had adopted new cultural norms and a new language for survival, but all that was native—Nahuatl—was not lost. After all, in order to covert Mexicans to Catholicism and to enforce their language of Castilian (a more accurate term for the language of Spain), the Spaniards would point rifles in the faces of Mexicans. In fact, many Mexicans watched their kin, neighbors, countrymen die—the ones who did not conform paid a heavy price. Thus, the Spaniards through the Catholic clergy molded Mexicans to their European worship, language, and lifestyle; however, Mexicans of the 16th century did not accept the illogical and foreign myths of these intruders internally. Externally yes. But, in secrecy, Nahualt survived.

For the next several decades, Nahualt Mexican Spanish took form; today, Mexican Spanish continues to evolve as languages do and because Mexicans currently speak a mixture of Nahuatl and Castellano—or Mexican Spanish.

The following words are examples: maiz, chile, frijole, papas, comal, pueblo, adobe, guajolote, tamales, piña, tabaco, cigarros, tianguis, oceano, volcan, cocodrilo, desierto, camarones, oso, jaguares, nopales, chinga tu madre, coyote, chocolate, vainilla, canto, algodon, Mexico, panocha, cacao, cacahuate, caca, cochis, plata, oro, jade, aguacate, jasmin, gardenia, turquesa, sapo, ranas, apupuche, champurrado, barbacoa, zanja, escuintle, papa, mama, cuate, cochineal, sombrero, amaca, teja, ramada, cerco, mazatl, venado, culebra, cougar, and the list goes on.

There are of course examples of Castilian words being introduced to Mexicans. With the arrival of the Spaniards, the Mexicans saw new animals, new plants, a new religion. Some of the words that were added to their language are: caballo, vaca, cerdo, naranja, limones, Pedro, Jose, Maria, Jesus, Manuel, Miguel, Jaime, Andres, Lourdes, tortilla, fuentes, padres, pez, gran puta, Gabriel, minas, and plaza.

What is important to realize is that in reality these words got adopted into Nahualt. The Mexicans took in these words but did not lose their own words as a result. However, because the Spaniards believed themselves superior, they bestowed credit to themselves for bringing forth a civilization. Except when referencing Spanish impositions, Nahualt and the other related languages were used entirely versus being forgotten. When the Spaniards did indoctrinate Mexicans with their superstition and bogus myths, the Spaniards had an upper hand at challenging the myths.

Nevertheless, geography would not permit the erasing of memory. Mexicans survived with the culture of the past although an accommodated form took place.

Later, when the Americans moved into northern Mexico, Castilian was being Nahuatlized. For the illiterate Americans, Castilian and Nahuatl was as foreign as Chinese. Americans did not have much knowledge of the world's languages, which was why they called the language of the Mexicans in Tejas, Mexican.

Quickly the Americans began their process: to Anglocize Mexican customs, they began to implement mispronunciations to many words in Mexican Spanish, the first one being the region they had illegally besieged: Tejas. Because Gringos could not (and still cannot) correctly pronounce *Te has*, they created *Tex-as*. To them, the j sounded like an x. Next, they transformed the identity of the Mexicans in Tejas to Texans. The Americans soon started to dress like Mexicans too—wearing sombreros, which had been in existence for thousands of years made from paja, straw.

These examples point out some true linguistic problems. Generally, people should not change words from another language and enforce their pronunciations. This is code switching as linguists say, or as Mexican street academicians say—it is Spanglish.

Spanglish was started by Whites who moved into northern Mexico. We see Spanglish everywhere: barbecue/barbacoa, co yo tee/coyote, ta maa lee/tamal, corn/maiz, va ne la/vainilla, dez ert/desierto, a doo be/adobe, Call low raw do/Colorado, Tux son/Tucson, Lost Crew zes/Las Cruces, Cal i for nia/Ca lee forr ni a, taa coo/taco, Sand Pee drow/Saan Pe droo.

Everyday in the northern part of México, the outsiders mispronounce the original words of the territory. The pronunciations for the Spanish and Nahuatl words utilize Nahualt sounds, which is why our language flows and sounds like birds chirping. If we spoke with a Castilian accent, we would talk with a lisp and use more of our throat and spit when we talked (Castilian sounds Arabic). Some people say Mexicans speak Spanglish, but we are only going by the rules imposed in school and by society.

It is disconcerting to know that many words in Spanish are mispronounced when speaking in English, but if you pronounce the same words correctly in Spanish, even when talking in English, people assume you are wrong. How is it wrong to correctly pronounce the words in their native language? How correct is it to use English pronunciations for Nahuatl Mexican Spanish words? Everywhere you look there is Spanglish, which Gringos created when they invaded el norte de Mexico.

The list of daily Spanglish used by this society is long. American society acts as though niggerifying Mexican Spanish is no big deal. The clearest examples of Spanglish in this society are in the names of places:

> University of California, Los Angeles; California State University System; California State University, Dominguez Hills; California State University Long Beach; County of Los Angeles; The State of California; Costa Mesa; Redondo Beach; Mission Viejo; El Segundo; Marina del Rey; Santa Monica; Salinas; Hermosa Beach; El Camino Community College; Mount San Antonio Community College; Occidental College; City of Santa Barbara; City of San Fernando; City and County of San Francisco; San Joaquin County.

The list can go on and on.

Ironically, the very centers of higher education are contributing to this ignorant practice of mispronouncing Mexican Spanish to pronounce English "correctly." The English pronunciation of Mexican Spanish presents a danger to Mexicans. When Mexicans begin to—and many have—use the language of Whites to speak and address, often Mexicans have reached the epitome of linguistic ignorance and self-hate. Sadly, this is how many speak, mispronouncing words and sounding like Brown parrots, with no linguistic literacy. English is cultural genocide for Mexicans.

Instead of being literate in Mexican Spanish and English, using proper pronunciations in each, the US and some US Mexicans prefer to be monolingual and virtually illiterate in Spanish. The tragedy is when Mexicans believe the English pronunciation is the correct form. Such was the case of an ex-cholo from San Pedro who said to me: "Camacho, man I can't pronounce it Saan Pe droo, it's Sand Pee drow." I felt sorry the cholo, for he defended the Anglo mispronunciation of the man who supposedly lets us into heaven.

There are other examples too. Some are confusing, some are misleading, and some are strange. Once, I saw a packaged that literally read, "Soy Chorizo." I laughed. Buying a new healthy kind of chorizo, made from Soy but was written in Nahuatl words derived from *soya*, meaning, to be. That for me translated to: "I am a dick." Somebody was buying dick without knowing so.

The ultimate example of illiteracy at play is: *Santa Claus*. The word *santa* is feminine for saint, and the word Claus is a masculine form of a name. How in the world can you say Mrs. Claus and believe it is a man? The correct version of *Santa Claus* is *Santo Claus*. As the Americans would have us believe, Santa Claus is a man dressed up as a woman or a woman dressed up as a man, giving gifts to children, saying, "Ho, ho, ho."

White Feminism

The Mexican household is a special and complicated place of joy, happiness, fighting, personalities, and memories. The household dominance depends on the personalities and makeup of the family: sometimes it is father driven, other times mother driven. Older siblings might have a say, but one commonality for sure is that the offspring have chores. We—the children—have chores: dishes, sweeping, mopping, babysitting, folding clothes, making the beds, scrubbing the toilets, gardening, raking leaves, and sometimes cooking.

In the household where I was raised, all the males did household duties. My mother would say, "Aqui no hay muchachitas, y a limpear." My mother made us clean, there was no choice and no sisters to help us. There was no notion of female and male jobs. All had to clean. Had there been sisters, then there would have been a gender division of labor, depending on how many sisters there were, but the males would have had permanent chores too. In my family's case, we washed dishes, raked the leaves, changed the diapers, and folded towels. In other families, girls had to do these chores, but I believe this always depends on the origin of the families. What part of Mexico (Mexico, meaning all of Northern Mexico with the part the "Americans" stole) they were from: rural, rancho, semi pueblo, pueblo, or city, Catholic or not.

Many times, the very mothers are the ones who perpetuate these gender differences. Many young girls resent this treatment. Now, as many of these young girls attend college, they hear lectures and read literature that criminalizes the household, the traditional household, the dominant abusive father and gender roles (particularly the roles assigned to girls).

I would argue this demonization of Mexican culture begins to take hold prior to college, in the K–12 system. These days, children are taught about physical abuse, not to tolerate and to call the police it happens. Some children have called the police, and as a result, some parents have lost parentalship

"Una Jefa"

over their children. In the vital years of discipline, (and Mexicans used corporal punishment at many levels), parents risk losing respect and control. Children have learned that they have leverage, and they use it as the educational institutions have told them to do. One instance I know of is, my friend Don Memo Esqueda. Don Memo told me that his fifteen year old daughter called the Southgate police when he was disciplining her. He asked the police if they were going to raise, feed and control her. By the age of 17, she eloped and had a child one year later. Don Memo did say that she wished she could return, but she had her own family to look after. Her youth was lost.

Teenage children want freedom from the strict Mexican households, and television and educational institutions tell them they can have it. Junior high female students want to wear short skirts, make up, and have boyfriends. Junior high boys want to wear baggy clothes, spike their hair, and wander the streets. Most of the time, the parents say no to these wants and rightfully so. But the classroom and the media culture indirectly says that their Mexican household upbringing is more than unacceptable, it is backward and from a different country.

Most of the current college faculty were educated during the rise of feminism and the subsequent villainization of men. Mexican females who enrolled in Chicano Studies courses studying women lumped all Mexican men as oppressors. A former girlfriend of mine who had graduated from UC Santa Cruz referred to me as an oppressor and being dominant. I told her she could not associate me with traditional White males because I as a Mexican male was also oppressed. Plus, I asked her how Mexican males could oppress White females, if White females had more money, more education, nicer houses, better employment, and rarely dated much less married, Mexican men.

What that former girlfriend and many other highly educated Mexican women fail to see is the power of the women. When our hummingbird approaches the flower for pollen, the flower can say no, the flower chooses whose milk to accept. Us Mexican men only want to swim in the pollen. We have to accept rejection, rude comments, attitudes, snobbery, sangronas, humiliation, deception, and change of mind with no consequences. Dealing with women is hard for sex and emotions. It may be easier to visit the Coahuila because there are less head games: an exchange, money for body, guaranteed release. Even the workers at the Coahuila (down the street from the Catholic Church) can say no according to a man's appearance. Us men have no choices.

And yet, we are treated as viewed through the lenses of White feminism.

The real tragedy of Mexican female education is that they start to see the mother as inferior, weak, insubordinate, substandard for cooking, and academically fictitious by utilizing patriarchal Christian notions of the mother as virgin or whore. The Mexican female begins to give up the altar of matriarchy. Prior to the arrival of Christianity, Mexicans and their descendents were a mother-based culture. Why, because the mothers are the ones who give life through birth. This notion is visible in mythology, astronomy, geography, and the animal world; the mother is sacred, as is Mother Earth.

Moreover, this has never ceased to exist. The mother has a special life force, though the father is not ignored (which is why the notion of duality exists). Still since because the offspring come from the mother, there is a natural and everlasting bond, for all of us have a mother. *If we have no mother, we are nothing. Sin madre somos nada.*

The mother is the nucleus of the family. The household is run by the mother. Of course, the father has a say, yet his world is outside as provider, teacher of outside skills, even the cook during the carne asada. An insult such as, "Chinga tu madre," will result in a fight: Do not disrespect my mother.

A weak Mexican woman, I have yet to meet. Therefore, I cannot understand how feminism came to the conclusion that Mexican women were weak. First and foremost, it is important to comprehend that marriage or having children is a woman's choice. Nobody forces her. My kind of Mexican is too poor for arranged marriages. A Mexican man who proposes can only proceed if the woman says yes. A Mexican woman, who got pregnant, does so because she says yes to sex, intimacy. Any other way is rape. That is prosecuted by the law especially here in California. When women get pregnant, it is because they are conscious of their decisions much more than men. The woman knows that if she gets pregnant, the pregnancy will only affect her body. If a man does not want to run the risk of pregnancy, he engages in sex with caution. When a woman does not want to get pregnant, she will have the condom available or is already on birth control. If a woman decides to have three or four children, it is because she views fertility positive. Some people would argue that it is because she is Catholic. This is absurd. If she was so Catholic, she would have observed the no fornication rule. Mexican women are conscious about pregnancy even at a young age and for many reasons: nature, someone to love, starting her own family, innocence, immaturity, and lust for the male partner.

In the college setting, young pregnancy is looked down upon even though biologically speaking, it is the best time for a woman. Even if the departments of biology, physiology or nursing confirm that women are most fertile from ages 16 to 26, the academic institution as a whole looks down at women who have children young.

Now there exists a situation where Mexican female college graduates are not interested in having children, and if they do, it is much later. Some object to having any at all. How did they reach this conclusion? Some say the home; it was difficult coming from a large family, quite comprehensible, but to the point that some women want zero children is quite extreme. The danger originates in college settings where having more children means being more primitive, uncivilized, or over sexualized. The Malthusian too many children argument seems to be coming from women and men who do not have any children (as I have witnessed myself).

The dominant society views men as providers and wants to make sure they are providing for their children, all men and women who work in essence provide through the state and federal income tax. In American society, 38 percent of money earned goes to the state. We do not have a choice; it goes straight there. We always work for Uncle Sam. But does Uncle Sam work for us? Do they provide 28 percent in return for all the work done?

Generally, most Mexican men provide for the family, but there are significant instances when the man runs away from his responsibility. Girlfriends and wives, they too sometimes change alliances or affiliations. The pressure on Mexican men to survive is horrendous. Mexican men do not receive White affirmative action. They are forced to compete for slavery wages with other Mexican men; they may find themselves becoming enemies amongst brothers and friends and sadly procure into this sense of Americanization and survival mode.

Laws and courts have assisted in the White Feminization of Mexican females. The wickedness of the courts is seen in child custody cases. The woman often receives favorable treatment at the expense of gauging the father. How many fathers do not see their children and yet are forced to pay them, the system? Haven't they already paid by their 38 percent contribution?

My best friend, Reuben Lopez, fell victim to a White feminized Mexican woman. While living in a garage and moving in and out of employment. Reuben's ex-girlfriend had a child (even though she told him that she was on the pill). Later, she promised to let him see his daughter only if their intimacy renewed. He felt she was being honest. However, she ended up pregnant again, without his consent. When he tried to be an active father, she closed the door again. He finally had the will to sue her for visitation rights of his children only to find himself slapped with a $20,000 bill because she sought public benefits. Although he paid taxes by being in the Marines for six years and when he worked at Goodyear, that was not enough. The county via the district attorney garnered his wages in half and suspended his driver's license. His ex girlfriend had no problem making sure the state crippled him financially and emotionally.

Yet, she is not held accountable for getting pregnant without his consent. If this were the other way around, this would be considered rape, and he would be in prison with one strike against him. Reuben explains, "Monica has no consciousness of fucking me over even though I am the father of her children. I have no rights. And yet she offered to drop any back pay support if I signed my children entirely to her and never see them again, because she is now a "Christian" and has remarried. Where was her morality when she was showing up to my garage at 7 AM on her way to her job, la puta that she is? She is a puta not because she had sex but because she leverages her ability to have sex."

After many conversations with the district attorney and a sympathetic employee in the office, he learned that by applying for General Relief, he could not only get cash and food stamp supplements, but more importantly, he could have his driver's license reinstated and stop the child support payments and interest from increasing. It is necessary for him to demean himself, to free himself from White Feminism.

Some Mexican women are quick to screw others over under the disguise of the law, eventually splintering our community. After all, who else are Mexicans going to marry if not other Mexicans? The end result has been the literal destruction of future peoples because once we begin to apply paradigms that affect our community. We become untrustworthy individuals, we have no one to trust in return, and we men become more vicious and less courteous. Mexican men have learned that a woman can be a danger because sex is power, and women have that power. My uncle from Baja California mentioned that his father abandoned him prior to his birth, but that the state did not go after him in the 1940s because it comprehends that children belong to the mother. The end result is the child is still a benefit for the woman. In Alta California, the state attempts to hold the father fiscally responsible because children are viewed as a societal burden. In Mexico, people know that the "jefa," the mother will always be the chief. The man did his duty by planting the seed.

The kitchen is the anti-Christ for feminism, especially if the cooking is done for the man. If the Mexican man works and attempts to meet his financial obligation, he deserves to be cooked for. I know of few Mexican men who do not work, unless they were laid off, injured, or fired. We Mexican men will do any job wholeheartedly if treated with respect and not abused. My friend, Ruben, works part time here and there; I teach at four different colleges, including at one weekend college program. We have a great work ethic. I remember the older men being diligent, out before the sun emerged and home with stinky sweaty feet when the sun set. My father deserved to have a meal cooked for him, and my mother cooked. She did her duty, he his.

Today, some female Mexicans do not know how to cook or clean. In the kitchen and food were the secrets. The undisclosed recipes of women lived, a place where men were not allowed. Women had their space because they fed the family. This was not a simple endeavor. This was how life was continued.

Maiz societies of thousands of years were exercised on the fires of sartenes, ollas de agua hierviendo y comales. This was vital. We rarely frequented restaurants because the best chef was at home. When we went out for dinner, it was to eat food not known at home such as Chinese or hamburgers.

We cannot lose such religious focus because food is God. No prayer will ever eliminate hunger as frijoles and tortillas will.

In the process of women "bettering themselves," they have lost home grown education for an Anglo White washed female version of laziness. I comprehend the need for survival in the USA. The USA is the ultimate survival program for Mexicans. Augmentation is what is needed, not the elimination of the home culture much less the superiority of the university. Are women better off knowing how to read a book through the lenses of White feminism yet not knowing the art of Mexican cuisine? Some advancement.

When women reach marriage status and they do not know how to cook, they should not get upset when men say that their mothers cooked food better. Of course, if the man is meeting the financial obligation outside to the best of his ability and cannot have a decent meal at home, he is merely an ATM, automatic teller man. I once read in a book about Mexican females where the author stated that the issue is not about washing the dishes but about respect. What about the man's respect? Because for sure, the hombre would not be able to get away without providing shelter.

The home is vital, and it begins with the kitchen, but this does not mean that a woman is subservient because she is in there cooking. This is the center of the house. We must not forget that, nor allow White women paradigms to dictate our future.

"A Student Waiting for Financial Aid"

$61,000: What Affirmative Action?

When I began college in September of 1987, I chose to attend El Camino College because a California State University or a University of California intimidated me. Doubt lingered in me; I wondered if I was I ready for a major university. What if the courses were too hard? I knew I wanted to pursue a higher education, because continuing life in Lennox and the fear of intense sun-baked, manual labor terrified me. However, in the back of my mind, I wondered: how am I supposed to pay for college? I saw the on-campus living fees, those fees were more than my mother's total earnings for 1987. I thought that $400 per month for rent was draining: a person would have to earn $250–300 a week and then pay plus utilities, food, car payment, gas, insurance, etcetera.

The decision was made for me. El Camino College was it. Many people mentioned that was a good place to start if without funds or specific goals. By this time, I was a cashier earning $7 per hour and was working more or less 35 hours (just shy of receiving full time employment, set hours that maximized corporate exploitation). I went along with this exploitation though because this was the best paying employment any Camacho had had in over four generations. My mother still earned less than $4 per hour at all of her odd end jobs. My first job at Boy's Market as a box boy paid $4 per hour while my mother earned minimum wage or $3.65 for some Korean owned airline food service. With my employment, my family had some more comfort, within my sense of limitation. I hated the fact that at my first W–2 job, I as a 16 sixteen year old earned more money per hour than my mother ever did in over 25 years of employment. We did not move out of Lennox, but I was able to afford a brand new metallic gray Toyota pickup. I would have much needed transportation for work and college. El Camino was a good ten miles south from Lennox.

Chapter Eight

As irony would have it, the semester I began college marked the last good days of state funding for community colleges. I was able to pay my full tuition at $50 as a full time student. The fees were $6 per unit but were capped off at $50, regardless of how many units taken. The real shock occurred when I bought my books, books that totaled half the amount of rent my mother paid for us to live in Lennox.

El Camino College was my affirmative action. The tuition was reasonable, one six hour shift paid my future. Proudly, I wrote my check and paid. I was not receiving a handout; I was working swing shift for my life. And the following semester, I paid my tuition again, proudly writing that check.

Sometime later, somebody told me that I should apply for EOPS. So I did. I submitted out all the required paperwork, although I was not sure what they really did. Weeks later, I received a letter telling me to talk to the financial aid counselor. When I showed up, the Japanese American woman sat down with me, opened a manila folder, and stated, "Last year you earned $13,000 which disqualified you from EOPS (Extended Opportunity Programs and Services)."

I was dumbfounded. How could I make too much money if I lived in Lennox, one of the most impoverished and dense census tracts in America? I believed I fit the profile racially which determined my economic status; I was a fourth generation Mexican Californio of Mayo blood who had a lettuce and cotton picking background. My father had died eight years prior from an aneurysm; my mother was widowed with five boys and had been getting poorer and poorer as Reaganomics ensued.

Reaganomics made Mexicans poorer, he "pesoized" our economy. A dollar was harder to obtain, people worked more hours and inflation soared. Regardless of what Wall Street economists say, when the rent tripled in a few years, going from $150 in 1980 to $450 by 1988, the side affects were excruciatingly painful. Mexicans in the US suffered greatly—a US devaluation of wages. We were those Mexicans who never lived in and rarely traveled to Mexico; we were Imperial Valley and Centinela Valley natives. I saw our backward progression; a guarantee of poverty. Poverty arrived like the supposed rapture.

"I made too much money?" I asked. We had Tepa x 13 decorations all over the neighborhood, including on the asphalt streets, but I made too much money. I was the first to attend college after four generations of agricultural labor; my father was a high school dropout, yet I made too much dinero.

The financial aid counselor did say that I would receive financial aid if I applied to USC as I had intended. I even doubted that. I made too much money though my English professor Wadsworth made fun of Lennox jokingly of course, but I understood Wetbackville and so did many of those Whites from the South Bay.

I continued working long hours, primarily swing shift, and then I started the graveyard shift. The graveyard shift was the most aching. I cannot think of anything more unnatural than to have to wake up at 11:30 P.M. to go to work. Staying up all night to work dragged on. When my shift was over, I ran home, showered, and then attended a 10:00 AM class. I would fall asleep in my anthropology class for 20 minutes, wake up, and then listen to the material. The instructor once asked me if I worked graveyard. He was one of my better teachers, for he understood. I earned too much money but only by working all night. I was not a whiner; I got the grades and transferred.

In retrospect, I realize that I applied to USC for the wrong reasons. I can recall my elementary teachers mentioning it was the best university. Years later, when I began to second guess this observation, I asked my Political Science professor what she thought of California State University, Dominguez Hills. Her Anglo Saxon reply was "not good." It was a behavior science college, whatever that meant, but I understood that it was like moving into Compton. Nobody would move into Compton in her White world. Thinking back, it was rather comical for her to look down at a Cal State when she was only a community college instructor. It was almost like comparing a Ford Mustang to a Pinto. Both USC and California State University, Dominguez Hills issue degrees. But in her eyes, USC was the school. And I fell for the advice.

The University of Southern California accepted me and offered me a 75 percent university fee grant. I would pay the additional 25 percent by borrowing money through the federal government, a Stafford Student Loan at 6 or 7 percent. I accepted, and by the second week of the first semester, I had a $4,000 debt. Simply by accepting the bait at USC, I could not afford to pay my tuition in comparison to El Camino College. I did not care though; I was at USC. I believed the arrogance, yet ironically I continued to live at home.

Once at USC, everything got tougher. Longer essays, 25-page research projects, $75 parking fees per semester, arrogant wealthy White students, it reeked of formaldehyde.

Soon after, I transferred to USC, I got fired from my job, and I reversed into the poverty of my high school days. Constantly short on cash for the basics, I lived off of school loans. I put an extra $4000 on my credit cards, and next thing I knew I was in debt for $12,000 with a B.A. It was at this moment that I wondered about the logic of going to USC, especially when I could have attended UCLA or Cal State Long Beach where my total tuition would have been under $4000 per year. I did not make a fiscally sound decision. I was in debt for the wrong reason—status.

The idea that going to USC will open up better jobs because of its alumni, I learned quickly was all bullshit. I was processing checks as a temporary employee for the Lawrence Welk Center. I was embarrassed but desperate, so I processed checks with a Bachelor's Degree in Political Science and one in Spanish. What a circus. Plus, I owed $12,000. No alumni connections, no job because of my USC degree. Only illusions of progress.

Seeing that I was going nowhere, I had applied to UCLA for graduate school. Once I was accepted into the Latin American Studies program (by weekly begging calls), I simultaneously enrolled in some Urban Planning courses so I could be admitted into a joint program the following year. Although tuition was cheaper at UCLA, I paid for tuition by taking out more loans. My debt increased to $20,000 to cover school costs and housing. I still lived in Lennox, but I concentrated on graduate school since employment was difficult to come by.

The Los Angeles County recession of 1991–1993 was quite brutal. These were the years that tuition jumped up sharply, the increases made by the infamous governor Pete Wilson who was taking advice from a senior crooked statesman, former President Richard Nixon. Governor Pete Wilson increased taxes, but more harmfully, he increased the UC fees. In all honesty, it was probably fair because the majority of UC students were Whites or Asians who have more disposable income. Why should they not pay more?

But for students like me from places like Lennox, Southgate, Boyle Heights, East Los Angeles or Pacoima, the fee increases were similar to extracting water from rocks. I subsidized the state debt through more personal debt. In 1992, I did qualify for a minority tuition program that existed at UCLA. Those funds covered one year of tuition ($1800), but after the cuts, the 100 percent tuition grant was eliminated. Once again, tripling tuition costs were endured, and I still lived at home in Lennox.

I did not care about the tuition or debt increases. I reasoned that I could work those debts later when I had a stable job. Plus, I needed to receive my Master's Degrees because I would not return to graduate later. It was now or never.

With no more tuition grants, my debt increased to $28,000 within the next two years. I had to borrow additional money because I needed to attend summer school and learn Portuguese. I had previously applied for this summer stipend but was rejected even though I more than qualified.

By this time, I was disillusioned because I learned most of the professors even the progressive ones where in all honesty arrogant, self-serving, egotistical, White assholes. Their academics were biased, racist, and void of real life. They professed to assist communities in need, yet I—as member of a community in real need—was admitted into Urban Planning with no departmental grants. The grants went to the student with the best GPA regardless of need. If my GPA had been based on my background, then I would have had the highest grade point average.

Mexicans from Los Angeles were rarely factored into the Affirmative Action debate. When I applied for grants or other programs, I noticed more rejections from people who professed to be of assistance. Many of those professors viewed the world simply in Black and White, (Jews were semi Black) and Mexicans were immigrants.

Latin American Studies was no different. When I saw who the recipients were of the summer language tuition, I became livid. One student was a white female named Margaret whose father worked as a career diplomat throughout Latin America. She was also married to a film maker. Thus, a white woman who was the wife of a filmmaker had her tuition paid and extra funds for summer school.

The next woman I knew was a Chicana who was married to a white guy who just happened to live in Malibu with her in-laws. She would mention the high cost of property taxes her in-laws paid, but I always thought it must not affect them too much because they continued to live there. I was upset because in the summer application, we were asked to explain our need. I explained every penny to no avail. By then, I understood that scholarship applications, at least for me, were a waste of my time. I had once applied for six different scholarships, attended all day workshops, even a fancy dinner where I had to wear a tuxedo only to be rejected by five of them. The one scholarship I did receive was for a mere $800 per year from the Mexican American Alumni Association at USC. This amount was a joke; one unit at USC cost $500. I should have saved my time, gas money, and hope.

Despite these obstacles, I graduated with two Master's Degrees and $36,000 in loan. After six years of higher education, I moved into the real world. I went through higher education without any affirmative action. USC did not abide by affirmative action, they were a private university. UCLA provided tuition only for one year before the program was abolished. My graduate admission was based on my undergraduate GPA of 3.2 from USC (Two PE classes lowered my grade point average because I received a C in both classes. Do not ask me how that happened.).

I went off to work, and six months later I was being billed for my loans. I paid some of the smaller loans off at UCLA, but those Stafford loans were killing me. I was being charged more money than what I paid in rent. I filed for bankruptcy and was glad I was not the only one with financial trouble. I saw people from all backgrounds in court. But the judge did not dismiss my loans, and I ultimately filed to discharge $12,000 in credit card bills.

Since 1994, I have worked part-time in various jobs primarily teaching. I have had to defer my loan payments too. I pay a modest $150 per month because my original payment of $600 is hard to live with. Still, according to the US Department of Education, my original loan has nearly doubled from $36,000 to $63,000.

The amount I now owe is equal to one full year of employment, and this debt only keeps increasing. I did not have any form of affirmative action, which I needed and still need. Some progress. Affirmative Action only affirmed that Whites win in higher education, as do some Blacks.

Affirmative Action affirmed nothing positive.

Inferiority Complex

The employment I sought was not intentional, rather by desperation. The first time I accepted a job, I did so because I needed to survive, not just to make money, to pay my gas, to eat, to pay rent: to survive. I began by teaching English as a Second Language on Saturdays. I did not care for the mechanics of grammar that was too mathematical, too slow, and too mundane. Repetition became my solution, the conjugation I turned over to the assigned assistant. My strength was conversing with my students.

My next teaching assignment was a course on Chicano Studies. My instructions came from my boss and friend, Marvin who explained: "Julián, look, the previous instructor was teaching about Marxism, socialism, communism, theory here and theory there. And truth of the matter, he didn't teach Chicano Studies. These students want to learn history, the Aztecs, the Mayans, the Pancho Villas and the Zapatas, the Chicano Movement. Theory is not relevant to Chicano Studies, facts and happenings are." Suave.

As I prepared that class, I thought about what Marvin said. What does Karl Marx have to do with the Aztecs or the Mexicans of today? Karl Marx wrote about Germany not about Mexicans in the United States. Later when I lectured, I saw that Marvin was right, students wanted to learn about the Aztecs and about the Aztecs, in the American setting. They wanted to learn about their place in American society and straight theory would not have served as pedagogy, it would have confused them more, as it confused me while in college.

I studied theory this and theory that, yet the UCLA graduate professors could not articulate why Mexicans were in an inferior position.

I would ask: "Why are only Mexicans working in the fields?"

The answer I got from an Australian immigrant instructor was idiotic: "Well, the Okies worked in the fields too."

"A Classroom"

Then, I replied, "Yeah, but the Mexicans continue to work in the fields."

She shrugged me off without ever mentioning that Mexicans were the original cotton pickers of California, picking cotton long before the Okies ever arrived in California. She pretended that class was the most important determining factor for being impoverished. When I argued that race was but without saying Mexicans were a race, she failed me. Ninety-five percent of the professors I had were White. And race did not matter? Why didn't I see White ghettos? Why were there endless Mexican barrios?

In other classes, my professors would refer to Mexicans as immigrants. They would explain: "Well it's because Mexicans are immigrants, they just arrived, they have to take the lowest paying jobs."

In response, I would say, "Wait a second, I am not an immigrant, neither is my mother nor my grandparents, they come from people who have been in California since the turn of the century."

Yet, many students and professors were immigrants from India, England, Canada, Thailand, Israel, Brazil, Connecticut, and New York. They were all strangers to California, strangers willing to classify me as an immigrant. This was the approach they taught.

"Don't teach theory, these students want history where they see themselves," those words rang. I had once thought the same thing myself.

By recruitment and desperation, I got involved in teaching. The more I taught, the more I expanded my own knowledge. I soon realized I had found a passion. I became a Mexican Yaki missionary by reading multiple books and literature. More importantly, I began to listen to my intuition. My intuition had been shut down while in college; spiritually I was dead during those years.

I continued to teach Mexican Studies at multiple colleges and learned early on that some of the other instructors perceived themselves to be better than the students. Better because they had a degree, more arrogant because they had a UC degree, biblical if they had a private university degree. I had many problems with that approach. Where we teaching to be proud or be pompous of a White title?

Then, I met a quiet man who always wore his hair long and talked about Mexicans being native. I felt that truth. I sensed that Frank Gutierrez confirmed what my inner voice sang for. And then at that moment, I sensed a higher calling: a career, to teach, to lecture in a way different from what we had been used to or brainwashed by. I stopped being ashamed of my Mexican ethnicity academically. I was told to teach from the traditions. The traditions that people consider backward, superstitious, inferior to westernization. Yet, knowledge was inner, geographical, verbal, and ecological.

After working at various part-time and temporary jobs, I was offered a one-year position to teach at a Jesuit University in Los Angeles near the airport. I accepted for reasons no different than my first teaching position, survival. My intuition was my guidance; however, I instantly began to clash with two faculty members, Mary Davalos (a half breed) and Fernando Guerra (an opportunist). From the moment I met them I sensed their aires malos, negative energy and the fact they did not really communicate with the chair Graciela Limón. That combination was my precursor, hijole aqui va aver chingazos.

Their first critique was, "He doesn't have a PhD" And that is true, I don't. Why shouldn't my two master's degrees from UCLA—one in which I wrote a thesis for Latin American Studies and the other I wrote a client project report for a local union? I had 85 quarter units or 55 semester units, almost equivalent to the completed course work for a doctoral program. Plus, my master's degree in Latin American Studies was a terminal degree, meaning there was no PhD; it was similar to an MFA in Creative Writing or Theatre. Moreover, I was bilingual while Davalos was monolingual. Her PhD better qualified or prepared her, but I could speak, read, and write in two languages? Where was the rational? The other critic, Fernando Guerra, could not pronounce many words correctly in Mexican Spanish, yet he thought that he was better because he had a PhD As all those Mexicans in Spanish would say, "Ese pinche pocho no sabe hablar." I believed Graciela Limón said it best, "Ese Guerra is an opportunist, he benefited from the Chicano Movement yet did nothing to fight a single battle. Y eso es triste."

In the spring semester, I was asked by the retired chair of Chicano Studies, Graciela Limón, to attend a women's dinner on her behalf and accept an "Educator of the Year" award at Tamayo's Restaurant in East Los Angeles. I was honored. I put on my slacks and Black blazer, which I rarely wore but for Ms. Limón anytime. I showed up and sat down at a table not aware of who else was sitting there. I was in heaven accepting an award, surrounded by beautiful women at a ceremony honoring Mexican female achievement, me a man.

When I looked around, I saw Davalos and the chair of Women's Studies, some Gringa. Davalos had the nerve to ask me what I was doing there, so I told her that Graciela had asked me to pickup up an award. Davalo's facial expression instantly became stoic and dumbfounded. I laughed inside. Although Davalos was Ms. Chicana Feminism, the retired chair and elder of Chicano Studies at Loyola Marymount University did not and could not trust another woman, especially Davalos to accept an award on her behalf. Of course, the incident only made her more of an enemy. When I mentioned to Limón what had happened, she stated, "Davalos brought that upon herself."

And to be gender correct, Fernando Guerra and his Center for the Study of Los Angeles was no different. Besides the words of Graciela Limón, an administrative assistant for Dean Kenyon Chan, Mariana Villa mentioned to me that Guerra's Center was considered by the Dean as "a joke." She once said,

"There is nothing worthwhile emerging from that Center for the Study of Los Angeles, we all know he does nothing but sit in his office." And yet Davalos and Guerra forced me out because Graciela Limón had hired me then retired. Their vengeance at her was through me.

When I wrote an essay about the lies of Catholicism in Mexico, I was told by the Chair of the Theology department, Thomas Rausch, "This is a Catholic University, if you don't like it, go teach somewhere else." But, I was not bothered. A white man in a skirt pretending to be a man of god is always an enemy in my book, but other Mexicans teaching about so called unity, then fighting to terminate another Mexican is immoral in all its intent. Not only by causing damage to another person but by perpetuating such behavior to younger Mexicans who will most likely model these people.

And off I was in survival mode. To another set.

This other set came by way of the hell lived at Loyola Marymount University. A man named David Maciel interviewed to be the chair of Chicano Studies at Loyola Marymount University. I spoke with him about teaching part time at his then site, California State University, Dominguez Hills. He was not liked by Fernando Guerra, who was heading the committee. I warned Maciel about the faculty too; then he went out sick and asked me to step in full-time for him. Somehow, someway, I was still a survivor. I taught film, literature, community development, history, colonial history, American history, genealogical family history, Nahuatl literature, and even a class on the border. Simultaneously, a full-time tenure track professor was hired from UCLA with a PhD in Spanish and Portuguese to teach Chicano Studies at California State University, Dominguez Hills. What Portuguese and Mexicans have in common, I do not know, but his specialty in Americo Paredes, and his interest was in Southwest Tejas folklore.

During my classes with the acting chair present, students would complain about the new professor from UCLA, not liking students to be late, or eating in class, or being picky with their grammar, or being mean and too arrogant. Students would state: "He thinks he's at UCLA, he doesn't understand that we come straight from work, we haven't had lunch. We don't understand why he is lowering our grade for grammar when this is not a grammar course. Plus he thinks he's all bad because he has a PhD he even tells us, 'Well I don't know anything. I only have a PhD from UCLA.'"

The acting chair, Eva, and I would just shrug our shoulders, every professor has his own style. But students would press on: "We know that, but he thinks he's better than us and he makes us feel belittled."

As positions opened up, I hoped my two master's degrees would be considered sufficient or equivalent with my teaching experience of over six years. When a new chair took over Chicano Studies, a professor from the department of Spanish, a new position opened up, but they wrote the minimum qualifications to include a PhD They could have written a position with teaching or academic equivalency. This would have made the search more opportune for others like myself; plus, it would have followed other departments such as theater or music who accept people with terminal master's degrees.

No, they specified a PhD even though a doctoral program in Chicano Studies had not been established anywhere in California. Furthermore, this requirement eliminated (and still does) most Mexicans from positions that have generally been known as "teaching colleges, research universities." They were supposed to be teacher friendly yet they were acting with a superiority complex, thinking that only people with PhDs could teach in Chicano Studies.

Since when has a person needed a PhD to be a Mexican? I thought that being born from my mother was sufficient. Plus, universities never taught me about Mexicans; in fact, they mis-taught me. From growing up and hearing my parents speak about this event or that event, I knew Mexican history. My mother would talk about how: her father picked cotton for the war effort in the 1940s, her tia lived through the depression when money dried up, my grandmother knew Cesar Chavez from being a lechuguera all her life, and my grandmother avoided the migra by putting on sunglasses. My grandfather talked to me about the Mexican Revolution, Felipe Angeles. My other grandmother would talk about what it was like to go to La Placita Olvera in downtown Los Angeles on a horse buggy from the Centinela Valley–Inglewood area to hear mass in Spanish. Moreover, from my grandfather I learned how books leave out Mexicans from local history. He would explain: "Ves, ese pinche libro solamente habla de los gringos y las Guerreros que, nada." I learned to annunciate in español from my father and how not to be afraid of dogs.

It was like my education of life. Literacy came from the family, and my degrees from the university, yet these were classrooms oceans apart. How could a PhD really prepare anyone for Chicano Studies? The tragedy was though many of these Mexicans (often barrio graduates) were acting like those gringo gatekeepers. We have been turned into our own enemies. Logic is not always present.

Academic instututions should not assume that somebody with a PhD is the most qualified person to teach. As it is, no university offers a PhD in Chicano Studies and only a few offer it as an undergraduate major. The racism dictates that Chicano Studies is a niggerfied degree, not up to par to White History or White Sociology. How could a university prepare somebody when they themselves have not been preparing a curriculum on Mexican Studies? If most Mexicans in the US are educated in English, then how would a PhD in Spanish be the candidate to teach in this field? Does this mean that a PhD in Spanish literature from Spain, Cuba or Puerto Rico can now teach Chicano Studies when these are geographies apart? If Cubans and Puerto Ricans view themselves as different peoples, why would Mexicans in the US be dissimilar?

A PhD in White History? A PhD in history is qualified to teach history (US History being a core curriculum course for all college students) even though his focus might be English, Russian or Canadian History? That is like saying a PhD in history can teach Black Studies because his focus is on American History. Blacks would have a fit. However, White or non-Mexican professors determine the pedagogy for Mexicans?

I have also seen this at California State University, Long Beach. I was once asked by a tenure-track professor in Chicano Studies who had a PhD in literature if I could help her out in prepping to teach Chicano History. Thus, we have unqualified instructors instructing and establishing guidelines to exclude people like myself who have equivalent degrees and have been teaching all kinds of subjects.

Sadly, many of these PhD Mexicans believe that their White degree makes them more valuable. They established their identity, while still leading spiritual warfare on others like myself and undoubtedly their students. They have an inferiority complex because they buy into White hierarchy. They believe letters behind names matter more than being a good teacher.

Zac de la Rocha's observation was right: "Know Your Enemy: they are the teachers who taught me to fight myself, assimilate, conformity all of which are the American Dream."

"A College Campus"

Double Standards

American society is made of laws, institutions, and a culture that allows for different treatment to be determined by the color of the person. In the case of Mexicans, many have not paid attention to color and its effects on those that are brown.

In my ten years of employment at different sites, I have noticed that Whites, Blacks, and Asians have been permitted to abuse their employment or are allowed to work despite ineptness or outright stupidity. The employment site is irrelevant—manual labor, white collar employment, the place matters little.

What I have witnessed in my years of working in academia—at colleges and universities, places where ideas are supposed to flourish and minds are to be working—is that there is a double standard at work. If a person does not speak and act a certain way, then that person is ostracized, shunned, and eventually banned. Forget the First Amendment.

In my experience, because of my different approach to history and political science (by teaching the truth), I have never been able to retain a tenured position. It is not that I am problematic; the problem is that I refuse to act like a cheerleader instructor for a society that favors Whites first, then Blacks, and then Asians at the expense of Mexicans. Once when I taught political science at Mount San Antonio College, I made the argument that the notion of democracy did not exist in the USA, since American citizens did not elect the president directly. The excuse of indirectly by way of the Electoral College is absurd and dictatorial. The US practices plantation politics at its best. Cuba and Mexico are more democratic, for their votes (or the majority of people) have a say in their national affairs. The 2000 election was the best case in point. How a man who did not win the direct popular vote became president proves my point. A small body of people elected the president. Let's not kid ourselves.

The next point I made was that the US has historically excluded the majority of people from the political process. Native people from the East and South and Blacks were never intended to participate in White American civilization. The fact that White women did not get to vote until 1920 confirms my point. The fact that Congress had to pass the Voting Rights Act in 1965 to guarantee the vote for people of color, to eliminate poll taxes and literacy English exams in Tejas for Mexicans affirms my position. In California, the political establishment stated that Mexicans could vote then gerrymandered Mexican districts so they could never elect to their Assembly, Senate or County Supervisor seat.

Before long, a White male student went to complain, and I was told to disappear. The bald headed White chair, Bill King, told me that I was late to class, but in addition to that, White students had complained (including a coconut Mexican). The complaints were confirmed by another Mexican student who warned me about their comments. I was not surprised; in part, I was relieved because I did not have to travel 25 miles to the east anymore, then back 50 miles to Cal State Long Beach.

What I found disconcerting was how quickly the chair wanted to censor me. One, two, three, four white students (and one brainwashed Mexican) had the power to silence my so-called academic freedom, my free speech. Apparently, the truth does hurt.

It was at Mount San Antonio College that I came across a faculty member in the history department who asked me about my degree in Urban Planning and Latin American Studies. I mentioned to him that traditional fields did not accept these degrees from UCLA, and he hid behind the "I wonder why" clause. I knew why, Ethnic Studies were viewed to be inferior. Yet, the White version of history is accepted blindly, even though they are wrong on many instances. Traditional fields do not cover the impact of Americanization on Mexicans. To state that the United States stole Northern Mexico from the rest of Mexico is correct, but they say Mexico "ceded." They white-wash the truth.

When I teach history, I cannot openly lecture about the great western expansion as a joyful occasion—especially when they slaughtered the tatonka or buffalo and dislocated Cherokees, Lakota, Choctaw, and Mexicans. American history must be presented accurately. The single largest genocide was the slaughter of Mexicans from California and the different Mexican Indians. And I am supposed to talk positively about this?

If you were to see my face, you would think different. For I look Apache, because I am Apache. Mexican Apache Mayos are southern Yakis. How should I lecture about the Apache wars? Positively? Every time I come across the images of reservations and dislocations, I cry because it hurts. Why don't

White professors state that land on the East Coast was concentrated in the hands of a few aristocrats and most Whites could not afford it, so they avoided internal revolts by moving west into Northern Mexico and stealing land from Natives, the Mexicans in order to award homesteads to Whites. Indeed, the Homestead Acts were some of the first Affirmative Action programs in American history.

At California State University, Dominguez Hills, I argued that White suburbs in California are the largest example of White affirmative action, and in response, the chair wrote a letter rejecting my re-hire to the Dean. Show me a White barrio in California. Whites have the best neighborhoods, the best funded schools, and the highest paid jobs for the least amount of work.

And here is where the double standard comes in. At California State University, Dominguez Hills, Howard Holter (a professor of History) missed half of a semester because he had a bipolar disorder and received a DUI in the middle of the semester. He was given time out to "recuperate." The former secretary Ineki Fike mentioned to me, "If you are White and tenured, you can get a DUI and still teach with no consequences."

Not only can you still teach with a DUI, you can be crazy and still instruct. A former student of mine, Eddie Viramontes who was enrolled in his class, told me that during lectures was either crazy or smelled like alcohol. In addition, he lacked historical competence, especially when it came to Mexico. According to Viramontes, "We would prove him wrong on Aztec history."

Interestingly, when students complained about Holter, the administration did *nothing*. As a matter of fact, according to Viramontes, they were sent notifications that they might not be given a grade for the course because they only met for half of the semester. Quietly, the dean authorized grades for all students, but as Viramontes stated, "I did not learn anything, what a waste of a class."

What's worse is that Holter was not the only case in point of White professors being given second opportunities. In the history department, there are also two white females, an Italian and a German Jew who act like bigots to Mexican students, and yet they are never held accountable by the administration. Lucciano and Garber are their names. Endless students have made comments about how White students were given higher grades on research papers, and if topics researched were not liked, then lower grades were given.

Considering these people are immigrants to California, I find it appalling that they are allowed to inculcate. How Northern Africans or Italians have been given the White ticket admission is amazing. Lucciano does not cover Mexican history in California and explains to her class, that Mexicans are not an ethnicity, but rather it is a citizenship. This means she knows very little about Mexicans. She even told a Mexican student to not write an essay on

Chicanos in Vietnam because they did not contribute. Her Italian nigger ignorance proves my point. It is a fact that 20 percent of the dead American soldiers were Mexicans from the US. And she is allowed to mis-educate.

Garber is a straight out mean professor. I could comprehend a strict professor; I afterall played football and wrestled, so I know the differences. But Garber was just plain vicious, a wild pit bull. She was the legal historian, yet while at CSU Dominguez Hills, I was the professor who was invited to speak at Boalt Law School and I was a part-time instructor. In other words, I was a part-time instructor, and yet I addressed the law school at UC Berkeley. Other Ethnic Studies professors from Cal had never been invited to lecture at the Law School. Since then, Garber died, ending the damage done to many, many Mexican students.

I can see the rejection claims already coming toward me, but this happens in multiple fields under different circumstances. At Santa Monica College where I teach geography, a student did not drop my class due to being hospitalized. I never drop students, for I feel I do not have to, that is their responsibility. If a name is on the final roster and no work has been completed, I assign an F. In this case, the former chair sent me a letter about this student, and I notified her of my decision. How can I change the deadlines and policies of a college? The student was unable to inform me in time of his situation; therefore, it was the administration's job to withdraw him from his courses. Yet the chair left me a message saying that I did not do my job and complained about doing extra work. But, that is her job; she is paid for these administrative duties. Later, I heard from my immediate supervisor in Geography that she whined and nagged about my not dropping this student because he had not attended. I was given a negative reputation, and my supervisor told me I was a problem employee.

Then, a new chair came in, another White woman, Vicky Drake who did not sign off on my fall contract even though I had been there for three years. I realized something was wrong when I went to pay for parking and was told I was not on the list. After a human resource call, I was told I was part of the late adds even though I was not a new hire; plus, I discovered that I would not get paid in the first time period. Meanwhile, my vehicle registration check bounced, and I had the state doubling my late fees plus adding a penalty for a bounced check. Was this chair to be held accountable for the additional $160 extra dollars I had to pay the state? Would she be reprimanded for her ineptness? No. I was stuck with all the late debt.

This is not about griping; this is about fairness.

Part of the reason that I have not been able to find a tenure track position in the community colleges or the Cal State Universities—although I have two master's degrees—is due to their minimum degree requirement. At most community colleges, in order to teach in the traditional fields such as history, a person must have a Master's degree in history, a White field. A related field such as Latin American Studies and Urban American History does not count. At Long Beach City College, I was disqualified from teaching a course called, "The History of Latin America" because I did not have an MA in History, yet I did have an MA in Latin American Studies (a degree which did require work in history to complete). Talk about straight racism. These alternative fields of study exist because traditional arenas where not looking at the role of Mexicans or Blacks (as in the case of Black Studies). A Black friend of mine, who had an MA in Creative Writing from USC was disqualified from teaching at LA Trade Tech because her Master's Degree was not in English. She had been teaching for three years, and suddenly they decided her degree was no good. I wonder if those student grades are invalid.

When the state passed legislation called "Shared Governance," what they established were minimum qualification rules on what is permissible to teach and who is allowed to teach in which fields. Another example of White Affirmative Action.

Good luck with being hired. It is easier to get to heaven than to teach full time at suburban colleges in Los Angeles and Orange County. As a result, power concentrates in the faculty senates and committees. By limiting who is worth hiring, Whites maintain control of higher education. The faculty has prohibited much of the hiring of graduates from alternative fields because Anglo Saxon paradigms did not prevail. Many negative changes for the newer breed of candidates have emerged such as: tenure being extended from two to four years, making a Master's degree a requirement. I have come across faculty members who only have a BA but are tenured because they were grandfathered in, including some Mexicans who squeaked through in the limited Affirmative Action era but only in places such as East Los Angeles College because in other community college districts, they don't even offer Chicano Studies courses nor have departments of their own.

At the Cal States, most departments are more flexible, but they require a PhD for tenure track positions. How hypocritical. Cal State Universities are teaching not research institutions. Once again, there is no accounting for somebody with two Master's degrees, but even worse, these universities have a two track system. Someone with a Master of Fine Arts degree in Theater, Creative Writing, or Dance is eligible for tenure track positions. I have argued against this unfair treatment, and the only response I have received is that their final project was creative. Is that academic?

Yet, I wrote a creative project in graduate school, as a matter of fact two: one called "An Alternative Proposal to the Puente Hills Landfill Expansion" and the other called, "The History of the Garment Industry in Mexico and Los

Angeles." These creative projects are bounded and housed in the fine arts library at UCLA. Why the *disparate* treatment? Social science creativity versus the creative arts: what is the difference? I had to create ideas and opinions: I created drafts on paper, argued, defended and had three professors' sign off.

Creative projects and contributions to the field? I have written seven manuscripts. Not all published. I do not control the printing houses nor will I write about how beautiful the US is. I only write reality: what I lived, what I saw, who I saw? No magical reality, only the rawness of life. *La chingada vida en Estados Unidos.*

Even in the writing world, there is this double standard at play. The only words I hear from Whites at literary presses are: "Your grammar is off." Nothing about content is said. The editor at Red Hen Press, Kate Gale, said the same words in a long letter that she wrote in which she specified the pros and cons of my manuscript, *Caucasian Tomato Packer.* Yet at the beginning of the second page, I found a few grammatical mistakes, mistakes confirmed by an acquaintance with an MA in English. My friends and students (primarily Mexicans) do not care when they see grammatical mistakes, they comprehend and grasp the message.

There is a certain freedom in speaking the truth, uncovering the façade and dispelling the "facts." All that I am saying is that we Mexicans are held to higher, unfair standards while Whites are not.

If you doubt my words, the case of September 11 in New York City and Timothy McVeigh weigh in. Up until September 10th of 2001, the typical terrorist on American soil was a White male in his middle to late twenties, who might have been in the Armed Forces or some militia group. We could even argue with all the school shootings—the ones at Columbine High School in Colorado and Santana High School in the San Diego area in which teenage White boys were out of control shooting their classmates and anybody in their paths—those were terrorists. Yet, where there terrorist laws established against the typical White male of age 15 to 30? Where there whole round ups of fraternity White boys in cities and towns of the US? Where White males in their twenties suspect in public places? Where they being searched by the FBI, Border Patrol, or local police departments? Where whole scale White militias rounded up and sent to Guantanamo Bay for interrogation and held without reason? No, no, no, no, no, no, no and no. In the case of McVeigh, he was tried individually and executed by the federal government. Yet, his accomplice has been given life in jail. But there has been no mass persecutions of White males in the way that deportation raids have accelerated on job sites in downtown Los Angeles, where only word of mouth seemed to be the only media outlet in April of 2002.

The English-speaking world of Los Angeles is oblivious to such persecution, the Whites are immune.

Mass arrests of Mexicans in the streets have been endless; for example in June of 2004, over five hundred people without reason were randomly snatched in Ontario, Escondido, and Bell Gardens by the Border Patrol. All legislation emerging relevant to terrorism has a stipulation of sealing the Mexican border. How Americans began to associate border crossing with terrorists in Tijuana, Mexicali and Ciudad Juarez is beyond my imagination? The majority of border crossers are US citizens or residents who live and work on both sides of the border. Every night on the news or CSPAN, there is reference to terrorism and the US border. Even Culture Clash in their play, *Border Town*, recently addressed the issue of falsely associating terrorism with undocumented Mexicans. Why would undocumented Mexicans want to jeopardize their future employment? If there is one group of people who should be more pissed off at the Habibs (Arabs), it is undocumented Mexicans.

Five days prior to September 11, an amnesty plan had been presented by President George Bush. This was one of the few times he spoke without his cue cards and that the Republican Party in Congress found themselves at odds over the statement of amnesty for undocumented Mexicans. Then, the tragedy of New York City and the new amnesty program lost hope and vanished into ashes just like the Twin Towers. Mexicans have a real reason to be angry at those *pinche* damn Arabs. Yet, the Arabs are more loved in the US. Public service announcements went out against committing harm to Arabs and Muslims. Muslims reached equality in religious discussions of Protestantism, Catholicism, and Judaism. Larry King interviewed leading clerics.

But nobody discusses the unfair correlation of undocumented Mexicans and terrorism. So, if there is not a double standard, I do not know what country you are living in.

"Mural on Marianna and Cesar Chavez in Los Angeles"

One Mexican Saint in 483 Years

In the summer of 2002, my grandfather said to me, "Van a canonizar a Juan Diego pero ni parece Mexicano." Juan Diego was to be canonized, but he did not look Mexican. Parece español, he looks European. My grandfather was disgusted.

I was intrigued. Most Catholic versions of Juan Diego resembled that of Chuy (aka: Jesú Cristo) praying before he was to be crucified. I always thought: "So much for prayer, if Jesús Christ couldn't save himself. How can he can save me?" Sin, the rational for Christianity, does not exist in my Nahuatl vocabulary. That is a Christian European notion. If it wasn't for sin (and probably alcohol), ninety percent of the world's population would not be in existence. Sin serves a purpose I call pleasure.

My grandfather languished in the hoopla of Juan Diego with certain disgust; however, I became interested in the 483 years. I kept thinking, 483 pinche años of Mexican religious devotion and donations, including our land and gold, amounted to one Mexican saint, santo. There were no good, hardworking, fanatical catolicos that could have been added in the Catholic Hall of Fame in Rome? Pinches catolicos y pinches catolicos mexicanos.

Where else is Catholicism more glorified than in central Mexico, where churches compete with the number of cantinas and whorehouses? Where else can men wear long dresses and not be considered jotos y puñetes but rather men of god? Where else can they openly discriminate against women and have the women accept the logic? Where else are the churches the most adorned, kept up, and allowed to still sit on top of ancient Mexican temples? Where else can churches serve as places of worship and yet attract thousands of tourists who want to view colonial Mexico, Espain in Mexico? And where else can you merge culture and religion as inseparable if not Mexico?

Mexico has a longer history of Christianity in its geography than the United States and Canada. Somehow, Chuy flew from Jerusalen to el cerro de Tepayac via the Totonac land of Veracruz . Had it been me, I would have stayed in Veracruz too: naked curvaceous robust pechona women, the best cigars, and jarocho music in the background. Veracruz is an earthly paradise.

But no, he somehow got to el cerro en el valle Anahuac and dressed himself as a woman. I thought cross-dressers were known as transvestites. Once in Mexico, apparently he addressed only one Mexican with the slave name of Juan Diego but spoke to him in Nahuatl. I didn't know Chuy could speak Nahuatl? Could Chuy speak Castilian too?

Then, according to the Catholic Church, Juan Diego learned Castellano in 10 years. Where there that many schools and teachers to teach Mexicanos Castilian? Did everyone learn it? But Chuy at this moment complete with his sexual transformation from a man to a woman could now speak Nahuatl?

I had a Tia Chuy once, she used to make the best atole. Mi'ama Alberta would say, "Vayan con su tia Chuy para que le den atole." Could la Chuy make good atole? My tia Chuy could.

As Juan Diego came in to the picture, so they tell us, the bishop rejected him. After some more wandering in the rose bushes, Chuy appeared again as a woman and left proof in a sarape, a sarape that had the image of not Chuy but of Lupita. When Juan Diego showed this sarape, the number one chingon, the CEO of the clergy, went down on his knees to an image reflecting an "inferior" people. This made Juan Diego eternal. He made Catholicism more appealing to the Mexicans than the Spaniards could. Juan Diego was merely a slave for the Spaniards, learning Latin and Castilian, believing this myth, discarding his existence. Then, he made his fellow Mexicans believe the paganism of those who were enslaving them. Whatever he did, Juanito got accepted into the eternal club. I wonder: does this mean that the Catolicos of France and Italia will worship him too?

When I debated the authenticity of la virgen, White students were amused at Loyola Marymount University while some of the Mexican students, especially females were angry. When I asked them if they knew who la virgen de Guadalupe was, they just shrugged their shoulders saying no. Basically meaning that some of the Mexican students were Catholic based on conditioning, no thought, just worship.

So, why did it take so long to canonize a Mexican? Did Mexicans not give enough of their pesos or labor? Most of the Catholic parishes in the 16th to 18th centuries were built off of Mexican slave labor. Plus, Mexican silver deposits made the churches in Spain and Rome rich beyond their wildest imaginations. I bet even God contemplated coming down and taking his rightful position.

The Vatican should canonize all Mexicans past and present. We have kept Catholicism alive and have enabled it to expand. We use Catholic verbiage, when we say good bye, we say: "A dios" meaning to god y "Hay dios mio" when something feels good or when in shock. The tone holds the meaning. Even if a Mexican is not Catolico, he still uses their language. Mexicans even imitate their physical beatings; if your mother beat you, the mission priests taught that. Don't be angry at your jefa, she was taught well. If your jefe drank, the priests taught him to be a drunk. They drank wine, brandy, cerveza when they engaged in their cannibalistic ceremony called the ostia, the Eucharist. That is why they slurred their words when in misa. Chingado, Mexicans even do the sign of the cross almost as routine as waving goodbye. If a building looks similar to a 16th century iglesia catolica, the hand goes up to the forehead down to the chest then diagonally up and across to the left cheek bone directly across to the right cheek bone, ending in kissing fingers.

I had a friend who would make the sign of the cross every time she saw a tower and red tile. I told her the building was a school, and then we came upon another similar building and once again the spinning of the hand ensued. She couldn't stop it; it was a reflex.

Once we passed a Baptist church, and she did it, so I said "Mira, te persinaste en una iglesia bautista."

She replied, "Hay ni modo, la intencion fue buena."

I just laughed at her confusion. She should have been canonized.

I do not comprehend Mexican acceptance of Catholicism, which is nothing more than Roman rituals and culture. At the entrance of most churches, words like: Santa Helena, Holy Roman Catholic Church in South Gate or St. John Chrystosom, Holy Roman Catholic Church in Inglewood are visible. What part of Italian or Roman society can be deemed "holy"? That is like American history, claiming to be democratic while Blacks were held in bondage and Native Americans were being killed. Italian men as holy interveners of God? Por favor, this is ridiculous. Guido and Luigi are going to lead us al cielo? Right.

Yet, their myths are everywhere they are accepted by masses of people. Roman soldiers in Jerusalen, not proven stories of Moises, David, and Chuy. Holy lands? Israel? Por favor, the bible consists of self-centered ethnic stories written for self-glorification. The Old Testament has no validity to Mexicans because Mexicans did not write them nor did these lies occur in Mexico. The New Testament is about a splinter group who deviates from Judaism. The stories are Romanized and are now sold as absolute truth. Superstition and pagan idols are the word of God. These lies have been imposed on Mexico and tragically Catholic Mexicans like martyrs accept them.

Nevertheless, for over 482 years, Mexicans were not good enough to be accepted as one of them.

I tell you, if I have to spend an eternity with Christians (Spaniards or Americans), I'd rather not live forever. I'd like to believe the afterlife will be a salvation from the wrath of Christians – and the Jews and Muslims too, it's all the same. Pancho Villa was once asked why he killed two Spanish merchants, and his response was: "For four hundred years, the Spaniards have kept us enslaved. It first began with their superstitious Catholicism and just for that they should have been shot."

The Catholic Church accepts nuns who launder money, priests who use machine guns, right wing organizations such as Opus Deis, and men who kill progressive human thinkers. The Catholic Church established the practice of human sacrifice known as the Inquisition, during which time those who ratted out any Mexican who was trying to preserve his traditions were rewarded while the Mexican fighting for his culture was brutally beaten.

If you are an Evangelico, Testigo, or Alleluyah, you are just as lost. If you believe in myths from the Middle East, you are empty. We Mexicans had—have—our own beliefs in nature, we just have to open our eyes: Tonatiuh, Ehecatl, Miquiztli, Tezcatlipoca, Mazatl, Xochipilli, Surem, Tonantzin, Our Mother!

Maybe my grandfather was right, they were making Juan Diego into a Spaniard. I wonder who the next Mexican santo will be. If it's the people, it can be any of us; if it's the Vatican, we might have to wait another 483 years.

Nosotros También Somos Mexicanos

DIRIGIDO AL PUEBLO MEXICANO NACIONAL

Hablo como de un mexicano nacido en California del lado conquistado por los Americanos. Mis padres nacieron en Mexicali, Baja California: (El Valle Imperial, el Valle Cachanilla, en la Colonia Bella Vista y el Rancho Schenck). Mis abuelos paternos eran mayos mexicanos, apachis del norte. Mi abuelo era de Mazatlán, Sinaloa, y mi abuela de Huatabampo, Sonora. Por el lado materno, mis abuelos nacieron en Guanajuato. Mi abuelo nació en el Rancho Jesús del Monte, y mi abuela en el Rancho La Libertad, a un lado del poblado el Rancho de California, ambos cercanos a San Francisco del Rincón. Mis visabuelos ya habían vivido en California, E.U. antes de que naciera mi abuelo Matías Segura Venegas. Mi visabuelo Tomás Guerrero, padre de mi abuela Alberta Guerrero, igual vivió, trabajó, fue expulsado durante la época de *Repatriation* y finalmente murió en nuestro sagrado corazón, Mexicali.

Yo también nací en el Valle Cachanilla, en el pueblo llamado El Centro. Hijo de trabajadores del field, pizcadores de tomate, lechuga y cebolla. Toda mi vida he vivido los desafios familiares, económicos, división social y territorial: yo conozco lo bueno y lo malo de ambos lados de la línea. Y he llegado a comprender que el otro lado, o sea el lado mexicano es aún parte de la problemática, porque los mexicanos del sur de la frontera creen en la misma división, en la frontera que los gabachos nos impusieron: una división artificial, una línea que no respeta la geografia ni las culturas mexicanas del norte. como la de los apaches, los tohono, los yumas, los cucapah, los pueblos, los mescaleros, los chicanos, los mexicoamericanos, todos esos pueblos mexicanos chicalones aunque no católicos.

"Mexican Flag Flies in the US"

Los mexicanos del sur aceptan la idea de que México dejó de existir en los estados de Tejas (el nombre original de Texas), Nuevo México, Arizona, Colorado, Nevada y California, todos nombres mexicanos. Este rechazo tal vez se debe a que la bandera mexicana ya no ondea en los postes, edificios y casas de este lado pero el pueblo nativo quedó en su tierra. Muchos fueron exterminados por la expansión Yankee pero no todos, y aún conservan nombres y costumbres como tacos, frijoles, mole, ríos, nopales, coyotes, calorón, desierto, tortillas de harina, carnitas, vaqueros, español mexicano, maíz, chile, casas de adobe, y las ciudades principales como San Antonio, Las Cruces y Los Angeles, que siempre han sido lugares habitados por mexicanos a quienes ustedes llaman pochos. Mexicanos no dejamos de ser simplemente porque hablamos inglés. Lo hablamos por sobrevivencia.

Sin embargo, los mexicanos del sur no toman en cuenta que las divisiones sociales entre los mexicanas fueron la causa de la pérdida del norte. Cuando Santa Ana pidió los fondos necesario al instituto financiero (la iglesia católica) para mantener el ejército nacional y comprar armamento, el clero en la Ciudad de México rechazó la urgencia. La Iglesia Católica prefirió que México fuera dividido en dos en vez de mantener el país entero. Cómo se puede seguir creyendo en esa institución diabólica que simplemente nos mantiene confundidos con mitos y creencias romances y judías que no tiene nada que ver con México y los mexicanos, excepto mantener un control imperialista y una mentalidad perdida en la colonia y la violación histórica?

México no dejó de existir en los territories ocupados simplemente porque la bandera de las estrellas ahora se mira en la distancia. El desafío fue y sigue siendo que los gringos se han comportado como bestias hacia el mexicano en todas partes: en la frontera, en los barrios, en los lugares de empleo, en los ranchos y en las universidades.

Ustedes hermanos del sur de la frontera nos llaman pochos porque supuestamente perdimos nuestra cultura, pero los mismos americanos nos rechazan porque nos seguimos identificando como mexicanos y porque continuamos hablando el español. Lo que he venido a notar es que ustedes los mexicanos del sur, especialmente de Sinaloa hacia el sur realmente no conocen al mexicano de este lado, al ser humano que tiene que vivir en dos mundos. Todo nuestro vocabulario y acento en inglés se basa en lo mexicano aun después de tres o cuatro generaciones. En Los Angeles, muchos chavos se hacen tatuajes no de dragones sino del calendario azteca, símbolo indígena de México.

Muchos de ustedes, mexicanos del sur del Bravo se sorprenden porque hablamos español mal y luego bien y al final realmente no conocen nuestro mundo. No saben nuestros desafíos e inclusive nos insultan, pero ustedes fácilmente y bien conchudos esperan las remesas de más de $15 mil millones de dólares. La mano de obra acarrea para México más ingreso que el petróleo y el tourismo y el país es estable porque no depende de bajas ni de alzas en el mercado mundial.

Los que vivimos acá también somos mexicanos y aun más porque ser mexicano en el norte es una chinga. Una chinga cultural, una chinga espiritual, una chinga racial, una chinga familiar, una chinga con otros mexicanos por ser la competencia. La vida en Los Angeles es para la chingada; no es fantasia creada por Disneylandia ni Hollywood con las estrellas del cine sino concreta como bloques de adobe que mantiene una estructura pero con el tiempo se derrumba por el peso y el uso.

En mis viajes por 25 estados de la república mexicana he notado que ustedes son más gringos que los mismos gringos y más gabachos que los pochos. Ustedes se visten como si vivieran en Nueva York, usan mas inglés en su español que nosotros y se pintan el pelo guero cuando los bellos de la panocha son negros. Inclusive, les gusta la música en inglés y ni la entienden. Que estúpido es eso, escuchar sonido sin saber lo que se dice. La música mexicana de todo tipo es más popular en este lado, aún cuando ha dejado de ser de moda. A mis amigos de tercera y primera generación que nunca han ido a México les gusta más José Alfredo Jiménez y Chalino Sanchez que a ustedes en el interior de México. Y no se hable de tacos y tortas porque allí no se la acaban.

Muchos de ustedes prefieren viajar a Europa o comer comida francesa, tomar whiskey en vez de tequila y caminar con sus perritos poodles, mientras que el nortemexicano y muchos americanos prefiere ir a México que a Europa; el tequila es el trago más popular en EU; la comida mexicana es la preferida y el "chihuahua," el escuintle de la buena suerte para los aztecas, es el perro más popular de los Estados Unidos. El escuintle "chihuahua" es el símbolo nacional y uds. prefieren lo europeo. Lo que sucede es que ustedes están bien perdidos y andan culturalmente más muertos que vivos. Ya se los llevó la chingada.

En cuestión de los acentos y el espanglish, es el producto de ser conquistados. Nosotros vivimos dentro de la bestia y la bestia es cabrona. El espanglish tiene que ver más con el desarrollo moderno que con otra cosa y lo deben de saber. Computadora, celular, televisión, Ford y troca son palabras inescapables que se desarollaron con el tiempo igual que el uso de cachuchas de béisbol en vez de sombreros. Ustedes mismos lo saben y por eso se les está enseñando inglés en las primarias y hasta en las universidades.

Lo que les sugiero a mis paisanos del sur es que en vez de perder su tiempo leyendo literatura pendeja de europa e irrelevante para los mexicanos deberían leer más literatura de los mexicanos de EU, para que por lo menos sean un poco más condescendientes y no insultantes con nosotros. Póngale atención a lo que sus familiares les cuentan y no se burlen porque no sepan español o lo hablan con acento gringo. No es nuestra culpa, es historia, y si ustedes no nos ven como mexicanos de California, Tejas, Nuevo México, etc. entonces se paracen más a los gringos y no dejan de ser hijos de la chingada, gente sin principios e immorales, que aún creen en la separación del Mexicano. Esa mentalidad va a resultar en nuestra extinción.

"Mexican Food"

Mexicans Are Not Latinos

During the 1980's, the face of Los Angeles was altered. In this decade, waves of people with similar names and appearances to Mexicans came to Los Angeles. These people were from Central America, the Caribbean, and South America; they trickled into not just the county but the whole country. There were several reasons: civil wars, economics, internal movement (Puerto Rico is considered US territory), and visas allotted by the federal government (every year the government allows a certain amount of entrances from around the world; this explains why there are many White people in the country).

The arrival of other Mexicans because of the devaluation of the peso would lump many of these people into the immigration status, but I would differ on this debate. First, the US stole half of Mexico where Mexicans had lived prior, but most never lost that historical and cultural connection to the land. Just because a new flag flew above does not mean that a place loses its identity. Mexico is a culture and geography that cannot be replaced with a piece of cloth.

Second, most Mexican nationals often headed north because they had relatives already living in Los Angeles or Fresno County; thus, the movement is more of an internal migration, moving from one place in Mexico to another location in Mexico. In many cases, families were reunited, children and parents, older generations of Mexicans and younger generations. Many were the offspring of Bracero Americans, those recruited to work in certain American industries from 1943 to 1964. I do not need to prove this position by way of statistics, I am the statistic. I have seen this from conversation with many Mexicans including my own family. The number of US Mexicans would probably be greater if not for the program transporting men south at the end of every season and not permitting the wife and children to move north with their father.

With every trip to southern Mexico I have taken, I am amazed as I converse with nationals who inform me that either they have lived in California or they have a relative who lives in Los Angeles, Houston, Chicago, or in odd places such as south Florida or Missouri. I was even surprised in my US travels to have met Mexican nationals in Overland Park and Lawrence, Kansas or in Muskogee, Oklahoma. Contact with people about their time in the US is also generational. Once, I met a blind man in the Delegación Cuauhtemoc of Mexico City who recited to me the places where he worked in the 1940s or 1950s. It was as if I was his linkage to his past, to el norte, the places he visited when he could see. I was his melancholy. Another old man in Colima shocked me as he reminisced about his years in El Monte, California. Wearing his tinted metal frame glasses, huaraches, shorts and white t-shirt with his sombrero, he smiled. Even in his pronunciation of El Monte, California, I could hear the correct annunciation and nostalgia of a past he enjoyed. I sensed I lived in an exotic land to the extreme north that is only real when imagined.

I have learned through these experiences that Mexico and California are linked for eternity while simultaneously severed. We were each other's linkage even though we may only meet for minutes. The young and old, I have met who have lived in the US often to return to their neighborhood, to their lives as before but with some more money to start a business or buy some land.

California is Mexico, and Mexico is California. This geographic culture is quite different from any other country to the south. This land is one with walls that divide an affluent White community from another poor brown barrio. The Tijuana or Mexicali borders are cynical notions of separations, yet every border agent knows that those crossing everyday are the same people who return at night only to repeat the cycle five days a week. Tijuana has millions of international crossers. All the daily crossings are US citizens or residents, not new arrivals. The fraud is the allegorical illusion of newcomers versus permanent people who are divided by an economic wall of convenience. There are no newcomers, these people have always been here. The newcomers are the Filipino, Black, or White border guards from Maine and Georgia.

This geographical relationship is what distinguishes Mexicans from other people of Latin America. The US is comprised of half of Mexico, the Sonoran desert proves it. There are no deserts in Central America or the Caribbean. Simultaneously, Mexico is not part of Latin America because of geography, and if it was, then the US would be too because they moved into Northern Mexico.

The arrival of the rest of Latin America albeit in lower numbers has caused an identity crisis among Americans and Mexicans too: Americans in California especially because a brown person to them is always Mexican; yet, Mexicans see a brown person from Guatemala, El Salvador, or Puerto Rico as different but with similar names. For the first time, both groups met Spanish-speaking Blacks, Blacks with Spanish surnames who spoke limited English or with a heavy accent.

Nevertheless, we Mexicans are still different based on our culture.

The institutions—government, schools, housing, employment—did not know how to reconcile this great confusion. The end result was a homogenization of nothing, the creation of the "Latino."

The term Hispanic had been in use since the Nixon Years and had more class than the inferior term Mexican. In 1983, I can remember my tio Antonio, a Vietnam Veteran who lived in Corona with a beer in his hand and carne asada on the grill, say: "Como detesto la palabra Latino." I did not know such term or what it meant. I just knew we were Mexicans and Americans because we were born in the US. I thought in my 13 year old mind: Why did he say that? What did he mean? Yet, somehow I understood as he smoothly gulped his cerveza that the word Mexican was at a lost. I saw him drink his frustration.

True to my tio Antonio Segura's comment, the word Mexican slowly disappeared, as if the word had no relationship to this space. As I entered college, the word Latino was used very loosely and the word Mexican had no meaning, no value, and no respect. Then, I learned that the word Latino was being utilized interchangeably with Hispanic, which I could not (and do not) understand.

As I came across Salvadorians, Colombians, Cubans, Costa Ricans, Argentineans, and Chileans, I faced instant cultural differences. We all spoke different versions of Spanish; many times, we could not comprehend what we were saying. Many of them used the word "voz," which to me meant voice not you, or they would say "vozotros" for us, but Mexican use nosotros for us. We Mexicans would never use those terms, but many of the other nationalities do. We speak with a different accent, we rhyme, we flow, we use Nahuatl words.

I have traveled through Guatemala, Honduras, Belize, El Salvador, Nicaragua, Costa Rica, and Panama and also to Peru, Argentina, Bolivia, and España. The differences between the geographies, cultures, food, and people are so extreme that I would argue our commonalities are rather minor. Even in the practice of the Catholic religion, there is a difference. I had to adjust linguistically to each country, and most of the time I did not succeed. They would always tell me about my Mexican accent, I stood out based on my culture and geography.

These differences must be comprehended to understand us all. I see as a true danger in lumping people together. When we analyze, language or words, we can see the differences between people who speak Spanish and the problem with *Latino*. The meanings of words vary based on geography and culture. Think about these words:

Aguacate: Mexicans in Los Angeles use this word for avocado; Whites mispronounce it as avo-ca-do. People in Chile call avocado, palta.

Barbacoa: Mexicans love to cook meat—especially outside. In Bolivia and Peru, they called this parrilladas, but they do not eat nor do they have barbecue sauce, mole.

Chiflar: For Mexicans, this means to whistle; however, other *Latinos* use the word, silbar. I was once denied a teacher assistant position in the Lennox School District because the White counselor stated my use of the word chiflar was not appropriate, even though 95 percent of Lennox residents are Mexicans.

Chile: Mexicans call a vegetable that is full of seeds, that will burn your tongue and make you sweat, chile. Chile may also mean penis depending on flirtation. Plus, Chile is a country in South America.

Cholos/Cholas: In the US, Cholos and Cholas refer to Mexican youth who developed their own style of clothing, lingo, or group identity in barrios throughout the Southwest; often, they are stereotyped as gang members. Territorial markings in old English font notify you of location. American alienation defines them. In Bolivia, Cholos and Cholas are the Aymara people who have moved from the countryside to the city and still wear their traditional outfits. They are looked down upon by the Catholic assimilated Bolivian middle class.

Cojer: Mexicans this word as a sexual connotation: to fuck pleasurably. Cubans, Spaniards, and Bolivians use this word to mean grab by the hand. I like the Mexican definition better.

Frijoles: Pinto beans identify Mexicans; frijoles pintos are a staple to the Mexican comida on both sides of the border. In Bolivia and Peru, they do not have frijoles pintos. I went to mercados all over La Paz, and the Aymara women did not have any beans to sell. Where there were some, they called them porotos and did not eat them.

Mariachis: This poetic music created via the sound of guitars is synonymous with being Mexican. It originates from the Cocos people in Jalisco and Michoacan region in the Pre-Columbian era based on themes of love, nature, death, betrayal, sorrow, and geography. No other country south of Mexico has this art form.

Merengue: This art form and word does not exist among Mexicans. This form of music comes from the Dominican Republic. People wise, Dominicans are Blacks, and Mexicans are not.

Salsa: Mexicans eat this sauce made from chile, tomatoes, jalapeños, onions, and cilantro. For Puerto Ricans and Cubans, salsa is a kind of dancing music. We Mexicans do not know how to dance to salsa; we dance to norteñas (Mexican ranchera accordion music) or cumbias.

Tequila: This comes from Mexico; it is the most consumed drink in the US and a novelty outside. In Latin America, there are different national liquors. In Bolivia, I asked for a *Kahlua*, but they served it pure and not mixed with brandy or any other alcohol. In Bolivia, I tasted *chicha* a corn alcoholic drink; in Peru, *pisco* is made from grapes. These are not found in Mexico. Another popular drink in Bolivia and Peru is mate de coca: coca tea (made from coca leaves) is an important drink to combat altitude sickness in the Andes.

Tortas: A ham sandwich or a group of beautiful women for Mexicans. For Bolivians, a torta is a cake.

Tortillas: Only in Mexico are tortillas found. Furthermore, Mexicans from Tejas to California (including Navajoas) eat these made of either corn or flour with butter. Once I ordered so called Indian Fry Bread in Kayenta, but I was eating a homemade flour tortilla like my mother would make smothered with butter. I saw tortillas de maiz in Guatemala, but I was looked down upon in restaurants in Guatemala City when I would order them. They automatically served pan, somewhat stale.

Aside from these words, there are a variety of other factors to consider in order to see how Mexicans are not Latino. As far as Puerto Ricans and Cubans are concerned, I cannot comprehend their Spanish. They speak too fast, pronounce their R's like L's and say chico and coño. I asked my Cuban friend what coño or pinga means, and he just laughed. Coño means cunt. I'm not sure what pinga means.

And what about "Che"? What does "Che" mean? People from Argentina use this word. My grandfather Gus would make fun of the Argentineans by *remediandolos*, "Che," and we laughed like hell with his theatrics.

Nevertheless, I feel more comfortable speaking to all these people in English because their English is much easier to understand.

Mexicans are different people. As George Lopez explains: "We are different people, even though the Chicano/Mechicano is from the US. Chicanos belong here.

We are different because we speak Spanish and get fined."

Mexicans can be defined by the following folklore of *chingaderas*: *Hijos de su chingada madre, chingada madre, chinga tu madre, panocha, pinche huey, pinche puto, puñete, orale ese, simon, hijole, loco, jotos, jotitos, huevon, flojo, cabron, a cabron, chingon, saquen se a la chingada, putas, chuntaros, nacos, perra, bitch, maldita, chancludos, pendejos.* To use the word, verga, is considered vulgar; el pito or el gallo is considered classier. We would never use the word estupidos unless to insult. We would never use the words: cerotes, coño, pinga, a la gran puta, pelotudo. When Salvadorians swear, we cringe and say low class, chuntaros. Mexicans do not eat pupusas, lechon, or arroz blanco. We eat gorditas, carnitas y arroz con tomate some call Spanish rice con frijoles fritos. It is Mexican rice (we are the only people who flavor rice with tomatoes and onions) and refried beans that we eat.

And we speak Spanglish the way we learned it from Americans by their endless mispronunciations of Nahuatl Mexican Spanish.

Yet, another difference among the people of the Americas and the nearby island is the difference in treatment by the US government. Puerto Ricans never have to fear the INS. As US citizens, they can move freely with no limitations. Us Mexicans who travel to visit family members in Mexico, even if US born get harassed when driving home as has happened to me.

Cubans prior to the Clinton Presidency were given carte blanche. If they left Cuba on a boat and were found by the US Coast Guard, the US accepted them via the Cuban American Act. Cubans have become one of the fastest growing immigrant middle class groups in the United States. Cubans are given financial assistance and residency. Now, they own the city of Miami; plus, they have influenced US politics-holding back the INS in the Elian Gonzalez case.

No asylum—economic asylum—is available to Mexicans. We Mexicans just work in the City and County of Los Angeles at anybody else's disposition.

Even Centro Americans have been given access to US immigration via the TPS (Temporary Protection Status) program after Hurricane Mitch. Meanwhile, 10 – 15 percent of Mexicans without US residency have never received emergency measures based on natural disasters. Hurricanes abound every year as do many droughts. Moreover, economic constraints affect Mexicans every year and those here as a consequence have not been given any form of relief. On the contrary, many sit in immigration prisons, many are sent back, and worse, thousands perish in the Sonoran, New Mexican, Californian or Texan deserts en route in the US.

In simpler terms, Mexicans are their own people. We should not be lumped into artificial categories with other people of Latin America simply because we might have related names or are linked by the same European colonizer,

Spain. Latinos do not exist because all people are defined by nationalities, cultures, and geography.

One out of every *14* Americans is of Mexican descent, not Latino, Cuban, Puerto Rican or Colombian.

Mexicans in the US are their own people and must be respected because the challenges we face are unique to Mexicans only. After all, we are a national minority, because the US stole half of our country and altered our future.

"Unwanted and Alone"

Unwanted: A Conclusion

As much as I ignore the border, that physical fence that kills my cousins and humiliates me exists, it tells me I do not belong. It makes me bow to the identity of American citizen, as I was born north of such division. Still when driving across the border, I get summoned into secondary inspection just in case I am not legit. Even their American papers do not suffice. They wish they could send me back, I see it in their faces. Never return, says the US border agent (a Mexican American) who feels entitled because of his Homeland Security patches. The warring border is real, that you know from waiting in the long lines to cross. The war never ceases on the US side.

After years of rejection, I wanted to belong to an Apache nation, mi Mexico, the one in which I was raised through my nino and my father, the Mexican side of Mexico.

I could not stand that fact that on my bi-yearly travels to Mexico D.F., I had to stand in line for entrance with obnoxious White people whoring in the south. I stood in line with blond hair, albino people with their generic English bland names. I was different: I resembled those Apache-looking people, and I wanted to belong to those people with Black hair, not those with bleached albino hair. Standing in line seemed like an eternity. I would turn constantly to look at the sign "Mexicanos Aqui" and the line of Mexicanos. I felt as an outsider in central Mexico. I wanted one of those green passports with the aguila in front, Mexico emblazoned with gold. I wanted one of those booklets, so I could feel I belonged.

I had heard that Mexican Americans could claim Mexican Citizenship. Prior to the late 1990s, even Mexico-born Mexicans would lose their citizenship if they had adopted American citizenship.

I set out to get my Mexican passport.

My mother and father qualified me; after all, they were born in Baja California, and were citizens of Mexico. My father is buried in el panteon Jardines del Desierto in Mexicali, Baja California. How much more Mexican could I be through my parent's birthplace?

I asked my sister who lives in Mexicali if she could obtain my father's and mother's birth certificates. She informed herself about procedures at the registro civil, and on a visit to Mexicali, we went to pick up my parent's birth certificates.

Later, I visited the Mexican Consulate with my grandfather in Los Angeles to inquire about citizenship rights, to get a checklist.

The first question the female clerk asked me was, "When did your mother become a US citizen?"

"2004."

"Good because had she become a US citizen prior to 1999, you would not qualify for Mexican citizenship," she explained.

Interestingly, I would not have qualified if my mother's application process had not sat unattended on some shelf in the Federal Building in downtown Los Angeles for seven years. US Immigration and Naturalization negligence saved me unintentionally, while they intentionally discouraged my mother from becoming a US citizen. The irony of life. My mother needed US citizenship even though she was born in Baja California or as people say in English, Southern California.

The border, the divide is right in the middle of my homeland, Apacheria.

"Mijo, why do you want to become a Mexican citizen?"

My nino, my mother. When I would ask my grandfather why he never became a US citizen after 60 years of living in Los Angeles County, he would reply: "Porque no quiero ser cuidadano de quinta categoria. Pues yo tampoco." My grandfather clearly comprehended why I did not want to continue being a fifth class citizen in the US.

When I would ask my mother about seeking Mexican citizenship, she would say, "Had I known this, I would have stayed in Mexicali. Your cousin, Liz, a US citizen lives in Mexicali, and now you want to be a citizen of Mexico. Even I'm not from Mexico."

I started to feel nauseous as the female clerk put the first *treba*, obstacle in place. I wanted to lie, but my lie would depend on her question. I do not trust any agency. I feel they alter the policy as they see fit.

The female clerk handed me a paper with a checklist that read as follows: official birth certificate of father and mother; your US birth certificate, Apostile from Secretary of State; marriage certificate of parents; Identification & Passport; The Identification of Two Witnesses.

After I glanced at the list, I said, "My father is dead, he died in Los Angeles County."

I was told to get an official copy of his death certificate.

Two weeks later, I returned with all documents only to be told that I needed to make two photocopies of each document listed.

One week later, I show up again. This time an older female clerk asked: "Do you have a copy of your parent's marriage certificate?"

"No, because my father died in 1980."

"You still need their marriage certificate."

"Yes, but here is his birth certificate from Mexicali."

"No, we still need the marriage certificate."

"But he is dead, my mother is alive."

"Pero aqui esta mi acta y la de ellos. Here is my father's, mother's and my birth certificate, they all match." Pinche vieja cabrona, vieja puta, hija de su chingada madre.

"It is not enough," was all she could say. *No es sufficient.*

At this point, I was livid even fuming, but then I felt tranquilo because I had legitimate, sealed state birth certificates from Baja California.

Weeks later, I went to the Los Angeles County Registrar Recorder for my parents' marriage certificate. If all of the paperwork was legitimate, I should get my Mexican citizenship, maybe I could even vote.

I showed up at the Consulado Mexicano de Los Angeles with all the copies, all documentation. I wondered if there was an American Consulate when Los Angeles flew the Mexican flag. I stood proud. I wore my sombrero negro, my black cowboy hat, the only one that fits my large, large, maseton head. I got inspected by security, almost a full cavity check, but I didn't care. I waited my turn.

The same old raggedy woman was there with her uptight face and her masculine metal frame tinted glasses. I handed her my documents from two different countries. Forcefully, she raised her Coca-Cola bottle glasses to review the illegible handwriting by Apolonio Núñez who handwrote my mother's legal birth certificate. He was the same official on my father's acta de nacimiento.

The haggard woman looked closely at my mother's birth place, and with an expression of rejection, she stated, "Rancho del Schenk," nodding her head.

I informed her, *asi es*. She could not accept that a Mexican rancho would have a name like that. Even I do not know where this place actually existed. It could be on the Calexico side, it could have been closer to the Colorado River to the east, directly south from Mexicali, but who knows? I never bothered to ask my Apa' Matias, I had assumed my mother was born in el Rancho de los Segura's right next to the Cucapah Ranchos. I even asked my brother, but she had no idea where this place was located.

"De me un momento."

Five minutes later, she returned and informed me that according to her boss, some consulate official, I did not qualify because my parents were not married when I was born. I was born in 1969, and they were married in 1970.

"What!" I said. "Que?"

"Esto no es de sentimientos, es politica." *This is not about feelings, it is about politics.*

Trying to control my anger, I responded: "What? I carry my father's name exactly like his. He was Julian Camacho, I am Julian Camacho. My father is buried in Mexicali, Baja California, my mother is still alive."

"Yes, but your father let you use his name, the legality is in him."

"But he is dead and I am his heir."

"He cannot testify to that."

"Y mi mamá que? What is my mother? She carried me, gave birth to me, raised me."

"Don't take this personal, it is not about feelings."

I felt like slapping her for calling my mother a whore.

"Mire señora, nosotros somos Apachis, indigenas de Mexicali, nosotros no somos catolicos. Yo fui el matrimonio."

"El estado mexicano no lo ve asi."

I was stunned. I did not know what to say. My parents did not abide by Catholic customs, we were Apachis, I was the marriage. But on deaf ears this complaint fell.

If I ever felt country-less, this topped it. I felt unwanted and not included. The paperwork from the estado de Baja California did not suffice; the legalized paperwork like the Imperial County birth certificate that signals I am "American" is also questioned, doubted. Once again, I felt that I did not belong to my geographical homeland. Two far-away capitals determine the fate of my birthplace, yet land is defined not by a nation but by culture. I had traversed through families on both sides. And, these two pendejos told me that I did not belong to either space. My Geronimo Nahuatl anima tells me I do every time I look in the mirror, mirate en el espejo. I always hear this voice tell me so.

I left in utter disgust and rejection. When I told my grandfather, he just shrugged his shoulders and said, "Mijo usted nunca va vivir en el sur de Mexico, usted es de aqui."

When I told two other friends of mine from Guadalajara and Guerrero, Don Memo Esqueda and Don Gervacio Pineda, each stated, "Esa pinche gente del consulado valen madre, usted necesita ir con alguien que conoce." *There were two problems: they amounted to crooks in office and my ignorance of their cultural lingo.*

I wanted nothing to do with seeking Mexican citizenship. Even though I had the birth certificates of my parents, both from Baja California, Mexico, I hated the Mexican side too.

Some months later, I was telling my Salvadorian American friend, Marvin, about my recent trip to San Felipe.

"Cabron, next time you want to go to San Felipe, let me know, my sisters bought a house down there, and they can rent it to you cheaply. Cabrón, my sisters were even given Mexican residency because they bought the property. The real estate agent arranged everything for them. When they travel down to San Felipe, they just drive through with their window pass with no inspection or harassment," explained Marvin.

I stayed quiet and felt even more depressed. They will give citizenship away to foreigners with money, yet those of us from the land have no access. I cried internally for being unwanted and not included.

When I explained my ordeal to my sister in Mexicali, she replied, "Vente a Mexicali y con una cuota de $70 dolares te dan la cuidadania sin problema. Las actas de nacimiento son de Mexicali."

As I heard my sister explain that in Mexicali I can obtain my Mexican citizenship, the words started to echo, sounding distant and hollow. I felt an emptiness.

I hesitate to raise my hopes in a land that is divided in half. The two halves do not want me. I have not gone to Mexicali, I am afraid of being rejected by brown people like me.

Bibliography

Acosta, Oscar Zeta. *The Autobiography of a Brown Buffalo.* New York, NY: Vintage Books, 1989.

Davis, Mike. *Magical Urbanism: How Latinos Reinvent the US Big City.* New York, NY: Verso Books, 2000.

Gonzalez, Juan. *Harvest of Empire: A History of Latinos in America.* New York, NY: Viking, 2000.

Harris, Sally. "Mexican-American Communities Remain Hostage to History." *Research Virginia Tech* (Winter 2002): 25–29.

Huntington, Samuel. "José, Can You See? The Hispanic Challenge." *Foreign Policy* (March/April 2004): 31–45.

Lopez, George. *Why You Crying?* New York, NY: Touchstone Books, 2004.

Los Angeles Times, January 2001–September 2006.

McNamara, Mary. "Rock, On." *Los Angeles Times Magazine* (February 27, 2005): 14–18; 30.

Pitt, Leonard. *The Decline of the Californios.* Berkeley and Los Angeles, CA: University of California Press, 1966.

Rodriguez, Richard. *Days of Obligation: An Argument with My Mexican Father.* New York, NY: Penguin Books, 1992.

Shingles, Richard. "Aztlán Lost: The Legacy of Conquest for Mexican-America Economic Development." Paper presented at the annual meeting of the American Political Science Association, Atlanta, Ga., September 1999.

Vigil, James Diego. *Barrios Gangs: Street Life and Identity in Southern California.* Austin, TX: University of Texas Press, 1988.